AMERICAN COP

Upholding The Constitution & Defending Your Right to Bear Arms

D0039351

LOREN CULP

FOREWORD BY TED NUGENT

ADVANCE PRAISE FOR
AMERICAN COP

"**Wake up America!** Our freedoms, guaranteed by the Constitution, are under attack! Loren Culp, the Chief of Police for the small town of Republic, WA has written this book to expose the truth behind his stand for the rights of all citizens, how he did it, why he did it and by what authority. This book is for real! It's not a TV show script or a book of the month story. Chief Culp brings to life our founding fathers' voices as they warn us of the impending danger we are facing right now! The town is small, right now his voice is small but the voice of this book is GIANT!! We must act now or forever lose our liberties."

– *Washington State Representative (ret.) Bob Sump*

"I1639 is a "feel good" initiative for the anti-gun crowd. Like Chief Culp, I have taken the oath to uphold and defend the Constitution in the military and as Mayor of Republic Washington. We take that sacred oath seriously. This book should be required reading for citizens and public servants alike."

– *Elbert Koontz, Mayor, Republic Washington*

For more information about Loren Culp's
Political Campaign or to make a contribution
please visit www.culpforgovernor.com.
Thank you in advance for your support!

American Cop
Upholding the Constitution and Defending Your Right to Bear Arms
Loren Culp

Second Edition 2020

Copyright © 2019 by Loren Culp
All rights reserved.

Published in the United States
www.olearypublishing.com

To get The American Cop Top 10 Gun Rights Fact Sheet visit
www.chiefculp.com

The views, information, or opinions expressed in this book
are solely those of the authors involved and do not necessarily
represent those of O'Leary Publishing, LLC.

ISBN-13: 978-1-7337104-0-4 (Print)
ISBN-13: 978-1-7337104-1-1 (eBook)

Printed in the United States of America

Cover Design – Christine Dupre
Interior Design – Lisa Thomson
Content Editing – Libby Julian and Dalton Fisher
Copyediting – Dana Mangarella
Back Cover Photo – Carla Blazek Tumbled Bones Photography

This book is dedicated to my wife Barbara who has been by my side through thick and thin for over 40 years and my grandchildren Isabella, Hyde, Araceli, Sy'rai, Ruger, Charlie, and Jackson. This book is for you so that you will always know that Grandpa fought for your rights. You should know what they are, exercise them often, and never take them for granted. Always stand up for what is right, no matter what, even if you stand alone.

TABLE OF CONTENTS

FOREWORD

Freedom is not free, and in this dastardly culture war raging across the United States, America needs warriors now more than ever. We the people who genuflect at the altar of the U.S. Constitution and the Bill of Rights salute Republic Washington law enforcement hero Loren Culp as a rare leader in this fight for the soul of our country by his refusing to violate his sacred oath as all too many others in government have.

There have been way too many flag-draped coffins to ignore the price paid in the name of the U.S. Constitution, and Loren Culp is a shining example of how our Founding Fathers hoped all Americans would be. Let it be known by all good men and women that the very integrity of this sacred experiment in self-government will be determined by those willing to stand strong at every Concorde Bridge no matter when or how it presents itself.

The America we know and love will stand or fall based on how many Loren Culps heed that call.

– *Ted Nugent*

PREFACE

"The only thing necessary for the triumph of evil is that good people should do nothing."

Do you know how to tell if an idea is exceptional? It will stand the test of time. That quote, credited by some to Edmund Burke, an Irishman who became a member of the English Parliament and was sympathetic to the early American Colonies in the 1700s, is over 300 years old. The war for justice and truth rages on still today as it did back then. And this quote is just as accurate now as it was centuries ago. I would guess that it will be cited another 300 years from now. Wouldn't you agree?

Although there is some debate about its origins, I salute the person who said it. Whoever lives by it has my admiration, and I count them a friend.

The truth is, I have tried to live by that mantra for most of my 58 years on this earth, and the inspiration behind that quote is why I am writing this book to you right now. As a trained police chief, I can't sit here idly waiting for someone else to do something. I feel it is my duty and responsibility to take an active role in upholding the Constitution and defending your right to bear arms. So you may be wondering how that quote caused a massive disruption in my life as a small town police chief and how a Facebook post I wrote went viral, and I ended up on the nightly news with Tucker Carlson speaking out on our right to bear arms? That is the subject of this book, and I hope that your time reading it will be not only enlightening but educational.

Picture this, the once quiet mountain town of Republic, Washington, population 1,100, where rugged individualism is celebrated as a way of life, where residents enjoy wide open spaces with pristine mountain lakes and rivers and where freedom with minimal government interference is expected. This beautiful place that I call home became the focus of the National Media in the winter of 2018 for what I consider to be a very patriotic reason, an infringement by our state on our right to bear arms and my choice not to enforce the unconstitutional new gun regulations in our town. Our city became known as a gun sanctuary, and our little town gained much attention. I will say that not everyone agrees with me, and I hope that if you are here, reading this book, you will keep an open mind as I dive in and explain some of the details about why I felt so strongly about this decision, how this all happened and why I did what I did. You might be surprised. I may change your mind.

ACKNOWLEDGEMENTS

This book would not be possible without the help and support of so many people along the way. There are too many to name in just one short acknowledgment so I will do my best to highlight just a few.

First I want to thank the people of Republic, WA for your support and dedication to freedom and liberty! It's been an honor and pleasure to serve you, I look forward to many more years. Working with Nick White, Jodie Barcus, Talon Venturo, Steve Brown, Elbert Koontz, John Lofts and Sam Kieser has been especially rewarding. I am forever thankful to former Republic Police Chief Brett Roberts for taking a chance on a 49-year-old rookie. Walter Johnson, thank you for the many late-night conversations about politics and life on the front porch. I look forward to many more.

I'd like to thank Army Drill Sergeant Maxwell, wherever you are, for your solid training and the discipline you helped to instill in me.

Thank you to rock and roll legend Ted Nugent who so generously wrote the foreword to this book. Your high level of patriotism and your unwavering support of the Second Amendment have you on a short list of people I highly regard as true Americans. Thank you also to Shemane, for your friendship and support. Please keep making The Spirit of the Wild TV show and spreading the word about the clean hunting and fishing lifestyle so many Americans enjoy and need. "Aim small miss small" and "where have we seen this before?" will never go out of style.

Thank you to O'Leary Publishing for taking on this project and pushing it out in such a rush. The Facebook post which threw me into the spotlight in November 2018 and now has me writing this book is timely and I hope the expediency with which we worked in getting it published gives this message the maximum impact it deserves. You are true professionals!

Thank you to Fox News Channel, One America News Network and so many other news organizations who gave me a platform to share a message that I so deeply believe.

Huge thanks to my family. My brothers, Randy, Kevin and Wade I look forward to many more hunting camps with all of you. My sons Nick and Adam, thank you for growing up to be good men! I want to especially thank my mom Deeta Drovdahl, you are my rock! Jim Drovdahl, thank you for being my dad for the last 40 years or so and thanks for taking such good care of my mom, from one veteran to another…Salute. Barb, you mean the world to me and I am forever grateful for you.

Let's Do What We Do!

Chapter 1

WHY WRITE A BOOK?

"If ye love wealth better than liberty, the tranquility of servitude [greater] than the animating contest of freedom — go from us in peace. We ask not your counsels or arms. Crouch down and lick the hand which feeds you. May your chains sit lightly upon you, and may posterity forget that ye were our countrymen!"

— Samuel Adams' speech before the Philadelphia State House

Aug. 1, 1776

I've written many short stories, most of them about hunting or camping trips with family, including some poems. I also write many police reports as part of my work. I enjoy writing and always have. I remember in school writing original short stories for assignments. I wish I would have kept them. My family has always told me I needed to piece all my stories together and publish them. I thought I would get around to it "someday." However, this book isn't "that book" and maybe "someday" I'll write that one.

This book came about through an unexpected and timely series of events that happened recently. Events caused by things I did and said at work as a small town Police Chief in Republic, WA and that is why I am putting pen to paper to share a message I feel very strongly about, and I hope you will too.

I will warn you. I'm not a professional writer, but I didn't want that to deter me. Most of the time life does not give us a roadmap, just opportunities to seize, if we so choose, and this is one of those times. So I hope any critics will take that into account as I try to relay this critical message to the U.S. citizens who deserve to know the truth about gun rights and what it means to uphold the Constitution.

I learned to type on a manual typewriter when I was in high school, and smartphones were not a thought in the minds of anyone yet. But we all had our Second Amendment rights protected, and they weren't being threatened like they are today. So regardless of my lack of writing skills or technical prowess, I aim to serve you as best I can. I encourage you to read this all the way through and then make your judgments. Here we go.

I am concerned about my state and country. I am concerned for the future of my grandchildren (all seven of them) and what kind of country we are leaving them. I'm very concerned that there are far too many citizens, police officers, and elected officials who will stand idly by and watch our rights disappear and our liberties go by the wayside, one little step at a time, if we do not take action now.

Some are actively engaged in the process of limiting our rights as citizens, hopefully not because they are evil (although history is full of those kinds of people) but because they don't know any better, don't care enough to uncover the truth. Regardless of the reason, only a few are aware of this slippery slope we are on and are also making a concerted effort to help stop it.

I genuinely believe that most people don't understand. Some might say that perhaps I am an optimist, but I find it hard to believe that otherwise reasonable people would agree to knowingly give up their rights and liberties if they understood the truth. Allowing the restriction of foundational rights and liberties protected by the U.S. Constitution is a two-edged sword. Even if you don't like something and are happy to limit freedoms in one area, it can lead to the restriction of your liberties in other areas that may be more important to you as well. It's the principle of protecting rights for all that is at risk here.

Hopefully, I can help change some minds with the information I'm about to lay out in this book. I know some people are so set in their thinking that they will not listen. Some won't even attempt to understand that what they are fighting for, or against, can be used against them in the future. That very thing is what our founding fathers warned us about. I will try my best to explain how wrong I believe this thinking is and help shed light on the fact that some of what we have been taught and what some believe isn't even true.

> *"The best we can hope for concerning the people at large is that they be properly armed." – Alexander Hamilton*

It doesn't matter which way you lean, politically speaking; this book will show you how both sides can slowly and systematically lose their rights and liberties they have been entitled to since birth. Rights that are given to us by our creator and protected by the founding documents of our federal and state governments.

If you are one of the people who voted for gun restriction laws, such as Initiative 1639 in the state of Washington, or something comparable in your state, thinking that it would make us safer, thank you for reading this book. I only ask that you have an open mind while doing so. I also welcome you to post your comments and questions on our Facebook page, Friends of Republic Police WA. I am on that page daily and would be more than happy to hear your feedback.

The information in this book is not taught in public schools nor the police academy, but it should be, in my opinion. This is about our history. This is about our form of government. This is about protecting the minority against the majority as our founders intended.

We are engaged in a battle. Albeit not one with violence, but a battle nonetheless. This battle is for the very heart of our country, its foundational principles and our God-given rights. All of them. Not just the Second Amendment. I aim to educate men and women all across this nation, liberal and conservative, especially those who wear a uniform and a badge and all elected officials who take an oath to hold public office and if this book accomplishes that, then I have done my job.

The police have a tremendous amount of power. The people I have met in this profession we often call law enforcement are good people, with no ill intent, and they use their power sparingly. Most go about their duties on a daily basis with no issues, even though some on the nightly news would have us think otherwise. But they need to understand what is at stake here. The police and sheriffs should be standing on the front lines, guarding against abuses, not just from criminals but from politicians, lawmakers, and the general public.

They can stop the abuse of citizens' rights—if only they will—no matter what form it takes or where it comes from. I believe a lot of them would, but are they being led by people who will, or people who even know what the right thing to do is? Their hands are often tied because they have to follow orders as given or make a decision to stand against these abuses and potentially lose their job. It's a tough place to be in. I understand that. However, as the saying goes, "You have to stand for something, or you'll fall for anything."

Those very people have the power to enforce, or ignore, unjust laws or make them. Yes, I said they have the power, and I will explain why. Those people can take away your freedoms, your liberties, and your livelihood, all at the point of a gun if they feel it necessary.

Once you have all the information I am outlining in this book, I encourage you to digest it and look at it from all sides. Then you will have a decision to make. Will you help to hinder or will you help to protect an individual citizen's rights? That choice is yours.

In this battle, we have people who mistakenly believe that the rights of others can and should be restricted (usually, but not always, involving firearms). Perhaps they weren't raised around guns. Maybe they believe the anti-gun mainstream media about guns killing people or the proliferation of school shootings and that limiting the rights of gun owners would solve these societal problems. Maybe it's because they feel threatened or unsafe around guns. Whatever the reason, they don't realize that the tables could be turned at some point.

Because they support gun restrictions, they are unknowingly opening the door to restricting other rights or liberties and ultimately having them taken away, too. If rights and freedoms, especially constitutionally protected rights (like the right to bear arms), can be taken or limited by the majority from the minority, then nothing is off limits. It sets a precedent that absolutely nothing is protected!

It needs to be clearly understood that if one constitutionally guaranteed right can be infringed upon by a vote of the people or our representatives, then all of them can be limited and restricted—free speech, the right to assemble, freedom of religion, the right to be secure in our homes against government intrusion—all of them can be taken away. On the other hand, we have the people who want to be left alone to continue living their pursuit of happiness.

The first group is more vocal, often seen protesting loudly, and sometimes engaging in destructive behavior, but almost always on the news demanding something from someone else. They demand tolerance from others while they are not at all tolerant.

The second group is less vocal, and they seldom protest. They quietly go about their business, working, raising their families and trying to live peacefully. But like a rattlesnake, they will strike when pushed and they are definitely feeling pushed with the recent passing of I1639 in Washington State and so many new laws like it in other states that restrict our rights.

I'm sure by my description of the two groups you can figure out which group falls under which political umbrella, although I realize there are people from both sides that would fit under either. However, no matter your perspective, I'm hoping with all that is in me that more Americans, liberal and conservative will realize the dangers in taking away or restricting rights. Even in the name of "safety," all Americans should stand against this abuse of power by the majority no matter what the subject or what your political party. Rights are rights and should be respected by all! Everyone should stand against abuses of them, especially those in police work.

We are on the brink of losing our God-given rights. They are being infringed upon piece-by-piece. Incrementalism is the gradual, small changes that lead to a more substantial result. The people pushing the small incremental changes in our rights know that one giant leap toward their goal would stir up patriotic, gun-loving, freedom-loving, Constitution-supporting Americans. They know they would lose or have a big fight on their hands. This is why standing against small abuses is so essential.

If you don't believe that some groups are working towards the total banishment of guns (by implementing magazine size bans, attachment bans, and other restrictions), then you are not paying attention. All you have to do is look around at all of the anti-gun legislation happening right now. Our rights as Americans are guaranteed to us by the Constitution. If you support all of our rights, then you need to be educated in the facts and involved with your elected officials, and you need to be active now. There is no time for pacifists.

If one right can be regulated as much as voters have regulated the Second Amendment and Article 24 (Washington State Constitution) recently, then others can be controlled just as quickly. All it takes is a vote of the majority in our current initiative process. What would happen if our First Amendment rights were restricted like some people are calling for the Second Amendment rights to be?

Maybe you don't think that would ever happen. Listen to this.

New York has proposed a law that would require people to turn over their social media history to the government before purchasing a gun. That is a violation of the Fourth and Fifth Amendments. Can you imagine turning over your records and paying a fee to the government to freely speak, peacefully assemble, or before you go to the church of your choice? How ridiculous does that sound?

Whether we agree with or choose to partake in individual liberties and rights shouldn't matter. We must defend all of our rights, or we will open the door to the abuse of others, all the others! It is imperative to respect everyone's rights, whether we choose to exercise them or not.

Restricting rights is a dangerous, destructive road to go down! Believe me. It will lead to our ruin. So when I say "our" I'm talking about The United States of America and all Americans. Our rights are the very roots of what being an American is all about; they're liberty, they're freedom, and we should all be for supporting that. So that is why I am writing this book, to help all Americans understand that all of our rights are sacred and should be protected equally by everyone, no matter their political leanings. If the majority can vote and infringe on one right, it can infringe on them all.

Chapter 2

THE INITIATIVE:
THE PEOPLE HAVE SPOKEN

"Those who would give up essential liberty,
to purchase a little temporary safety,
deserve neither liberty nor safety."
— Benjamin Franklin

Let's take a look at the initiative that was recently passed in Washington State, the infringements that it includes and what started the media interest and the controversy that inspired me to write this book. Roughly half of the states in the United States have an initiative process where citizens can initiate a law by getting enough signatures to get a proposed law on the ballot. It can then become law once it has qualified to be on the ballot and the majority of voters approve it.

Any citizen can propose any initiative, and it will be on the ballot if they can gather enough signatures.

The media is then used to persuade voters one way or another. Often the group that has the most money for advertising wins. It is direct democracy in action but is it a good thing?

On November 6, 2018 voters in Washington State approved Initiative 1639, otherwise known as The Public Safety and Semiautomatic Rifle Act. This act does what one of our founding fathers, Benjamin Franklin, warned about in the above quote. Those in favor of it want us all to give up liberty in the name of safety.

The initiative, all thirty pages of it, does several things including, but not limited to:

- **All semi-automatic rifles are now called "assault weapons."**

  Assault is an action; it is not a weapon. To assault someone is a crime. Period. Firearms are used most frequently for defensive protection, but you won't hear about most of those events on the mainstream media because it doesn't fit their agenda. Calling firearms "defensive weapons" doesn't fit the agenda either; that's why they came up with the name "Assault Weapons." It sounds scary. Why? No one wants to be assaulted. However, people have used knives, rocks, cars, pills, poison, ropes and just about everything else to kill other people. Should we also add assault to the beginning of those words?

  Why don't we start calling vehicles "assault cars," because more people are killed by the use of cars than are killed by the use of firearms every year? If it's about saving lives, then maybe we should ban cars?

FBI Crime Data shows that in 2017 there were 403 people killed with rifles of all types: bolt action, lever action, and others. That same year 467 were killed with blunt force objects: hammers, clubs, and other objects. There were 692 people murdered with personal weapons: hands, fists, and feet. Almost twice the number were killed with no weapon at all! So it's clear that the word "assault" has an agenda behind it.

- **Bans the sale of "assault weapons" to anyone under 21 years old.**

I joined the U.S. Military at the age of 19, and I traveled halfway around the world in defense of our country. I also attended the Drill Sergeant School at Fort Leonard Wood, Missouri. As a Drill Corporal, I trained hundreds of combat engineers on some of the most advanced weapons in the world.

Many people join the military at the age of 17 or 18, to the tune of hundreds of thousands of people. It makes no sense that young people can join the military and go off to defend our country using some of the most advanced weapons systems in the world, but when they come home they can't exercise the very rights they are supposedly fighting for? How is that justice?

- **Requires background checks and approval from a sheriff or chief.**

  What other constitutionally protected rights would anyone be okay with having to ask a government official for permission to exercise? The Constitution restricts the government, not citizens. Read the first sentence in the First Amendment; 'Congress shall make no law.' Why would we as citizens need to ask permission from a government official for something we were given at birth? Where do we get our rights? If you answered, "from the government," you are wrong. We get our rights from God.

- **Requires government inspections of your private medical records.**

  This is a violation of the Fourth and Fifth Amendments against search and seizure without a warrant and self-incrimination. The Fourth Amendment is very clear and says you should be secure in your homes, persons, papers, and effects and, without a warrant, sworn to by an officer and signed by an impartial judge, the government needs to leave us alone. The government has no right to look at any of "your papers" without a warrant, and that includes medical records. This proposed (and passed) initiative is in direct violation of our Constitution.

  U.S. Constitution Article IV:

  "The right of the people to be secure in their persons, houses, papers, and effects, against unreasonable searches and seizures, shall not be violated, and no Warrants shall issue, but upon probable cause, supported by Oath or affirmation, and particularly describing the place to be searched, and the persons or things to be seized."

The Fifth Amendment clearly states that a person should not have to be a witness against themselves.

U.S. Constitution Article V:

"No person shall be held to answer for a capital, or otherwise infamous crime, unless on a presentment or indictment of a Grand Jury, except in cases arising in the land or naval forces, or in the Militia, when in actual service in time of War or public danger; nor shall any person be subject for the same offence to be twice put in jeopardy of life or limb; nor shall be compelled in any criminal case to be a witness against himself, nor be deprived of life, liberty, or property, without due process of law; nor shall private property be taken for public use, without just compensation."

Let's keep going. If all that isn't enough to convince you yet, here are more restrictions that were passed in Initiative 1639:

- **Requires paying a fee to the State.**

What other constitutionally protected rights would anyone be ok with having to pay a fee to the government to exercise? Should the government charge us for exercising the First Amendment? What if you couldn't afford to pay for free speech? Should your rights to free speech be taken away or limited? It seems ridiculous, doesn't it? Because it is!

- **Requires proof of training every five years for purchases.**

  How would you feel about having to complete government training in speaking before you could exercise your First Amendment rights? I could use some training in public speaking, but I don't want to be required to do so and pay a fee to the government. That's also silly, right?

- **Can make you a felon if your gun is stolen and used in a crime.**

  If a criminal breaks into your home and steals a firearm and then commits a crime with that firearm, you as the gun owner can be charged with up to a felony. So, using that logic, if someone steals your car and runs through a crowd of people, would you be okay with the government charging you, as the owner of the vehicle, with a felony? That's what this initiative proposes to do to lawful gun owners.

This initiative is for a little perceived safety, by limiting gun rights for law-abiding citizens. However, it will do nothing to stop criminals. Why? Because criminals do not follow laws. Does that come as a surprise to you? That's what makes them criminals. Only law-abiding citizens obey the law, so this law only affects the law-abiding, gun-carrying citizens. Criminals will do what criminals do: ignore the laws and commit crimes.

Trust me. I know this from firsthand experience. After all, I am a cop! If laws stopped criminals and those with evil intent from committing crimes, then we would not need the police. Yet I deal with crime every day at work. I arrest people who break laws and harm or try to harm others. No new law is going to change that.

There are already thousands of laws, and I am grateful for the continued progress we have made as a country since our founding over 200 years ago, but how many more do we need? Are we willing to open the door to more laws that will further restrict the freedoms that we have been given and the core values that make our country so great? I, for one, do not think it is wise.

Am I calling for abolishing laws? Absolutely not! Laws are necessary to keep order. Laws are in place to punish criminals but should not be used to make otherwise law-abiding citizens, who are exercising their rights, into criminals!

Initiative 1639 (also known as I1639) was approved by a majority of the popular vote. Approximately 60% of the people voted for it. If we break that vote down by county, the majority of the counties in Washington State voted against the initiative (25 counties were against), and only 14 counties voted for it.

This initiative was presented "by the people" for a vote to "increase public safety and reduce gun violence." Sounds great! Who doesn't want increased public safety and less violence? That's where misleading advertising comes into play. Convincing the public that restricting guns is a move towards a safer society may seem like common sense. But is it?

I'm sure many people who voted for this initiative are well-meaning people who think fewer guns equal a safer world. However, they genuinely lack the understanding of what the initiative does, whom it will affect and how little it will change any public safety concerns. Maybe you are one of those people who was misled by the proponents of this initiative or one that is similar to this in your state. Keep reading. I promise to break it down even further for you.

"I was recently asked by a young supporter of this initiative in Seattle, via email, "What would happen if someone bought a gun in Republic and went to Seattle and killed a bunch of people?" Great question! My answer to that person was a question of my own, "What if someone bought a car in Seattle and drove it over to Republic and ran over a bunch of people?"

Both are criminal offenses, and the person responsible for committing the crime should be punished, not everyone who owns a gun and not everyone who owns a car. That to me is common sense. Although I never got a reply back, I appreciated the interest and the activism. I understand it's hard to talk about politically-charged topics in our culture today without getting angry and pointing fingers. I also know that the only way we are going to unite and uphold our great country is to ask tough questions, listen to reason and be willing to uncover the truth, rather than believing media hype and fear-based propaganda.

Before this initiative passed, I took the time to read it. I encourage you to do the same before you vote on anything. It's surprising how many people vote on issues they do not understand or have not taken the time to research themselves. After reading the whole proposal, and based on my values to uphold the Constitution, I made an informed decision that I would vote against it. I felt that most of my fellow Washingtonians would do the same. In fact, I thought there was no way the voters in Washington State would pass it! I've lived here all of my life, except the time when I served our country in the military. Much to my surprise, it passed.

On November 7, 2018, the day after the initiative passed, I was at work in the City of Republic as the Police Chief. I was approached by a concerned citizen who asked me if we, the police, were going to start arresting people under 21 who might have a semi-automatic rifle in their possession. I assured this person that I would not arrest anyone because it would be a violation of their constitutional rights.

That day several other people asked me the same question, and I gave the same answer. I've taken an oath, not just once but three times to 'uphold and defend

Sergeant Culp being sworn in as Chief of Police by Mayor Koontz 2016.

the Constitution of the United States and the Washington State Constitution.' I don't take that oath lightly.

Although Republic is a small town, we have the same problems as bigger cities but on a smaller scale. We have rapes, burglaries, child abuse, drugs, thefts, assaults and the like. The difference is, we, like thousands of small cities and towns all across the country, don't have specialized units. There is no detective bureau to hand a case off to, no DUI (Driving Under the Influence) unit, no specialized units at all. We are the specialists. We do it all. We take a case from beginning to end. Because of budget cuts, our department has been reduced, from a three-man force with a secretary to a two-man force with no secretary. As a working chief with a caseload, I have things to do other than talk to people all day about an initiative. So I decided to make my position known to all the citizens of Republic the best way I knew how, on Facebook. Little did I know that decision would not have a small reaction.

Chapter 3

THE POST THAT WAS HEARD 'ROUND THE WORLD

"No man shall ever be debarred the use of arms. The strongest reason for the people to retain the right to keep and bear arms is, as a last resort, to protect themselves against the tyranny in government."
– Thomas Jefferson

"To disarm the people is the best and most effective way to enslave them..." – George Mason

Located in the northeastern part of the state lies the City of Republic. We are less than a half hour from the Canadian border and surrounded by beautiful mountains covered in trees, open meadows and rock outcroppings. It is an outdoor-person's dream destination. Hundreds of people come here during hunting season to get a great chance at taking some good clean meat home for the freezer.

People visiting during the summer enjoy all of the lakes, rivers, and scenery. Water skiing, fishing, horseback riding, hiking, biking or just hanging out at one of the many resorts is a big draw for people who want to "get away from it all."

In the winter there are other outdoor activities to enjoy. Winter sports, like cross country skiing, snowmobiling and Winter Fest in January, where a city block is closed off in downtown Republic for the outhouse races and sculptures in the snow, draws many people from outside areas.

Archery and rifle seasons are busy times for local businesses as well. Hunters and their families come for the abundant whitetail and mule deer in the area, with the hope of filling the freezer. It is not uncommon for other officers and me to encounter guns in a vehicle any time of the year, especially during hunting season. This is AMERICA and owning a gun and carrying it is not against the law.

Our sleepy town got a lot of national attention recently. I can assure you it wasn't something I planned or that even crossed my mind, and yet, I am grateful for the opportunity to be a voice of reason and serve our country at this time in history when our rights are being jeopardized. It all started with the "post heard 'round the world." Let me explain what happened.

One way that most police departments communicate with the citizens they work for is with social media. It is a great way to get information out to most of the public in a rapid fashion. Whether it's posting about a wanted person, crimes that are happening in the area or just local information that is important to our citizens in general, social media has created a vehicle for communication that is simple and effective. A lot of people use it and like it.

So, following the questions and concerns I received after the passing of Initiative 1639, I made a post on my Facebook page, Friends of Republic Police WA to get the word out to the citizens of Republic about where I stood on gun rights. Although our Facebook following was small, roughly the size of our population at 1,000 people, I felt it was the right thing to do to put them all at ease. I posted the following message to the citizens of Republic:

"I've talked to quite a few concerned citizens today so let me clear something up.

I've taken three public oaths, one in the U.S. Army and two as a police officer. All of them included upholding and defending the Constitution of the United States of America.

The Second Amendment says the right to keep and bear arms shall not be infringed.

As long as I am Chief of Police, no Republic Police Officer will infringe on a citizen's right to keep and bear arms, PERIOD! – Chief Culp"

The purpose of the post was to leave no doubt in the minds of the people of Republic where I stood. There was no way we were going to violate people's constitutional rights while doing our jobs and I wanted people to know that there is no way I would arrest them for not giving up their constitutional right to bear arms.

Adam Culp giving 8 year old Daughter Charlie firearm lessons.

I learned to shoot at a young age. I got my first deer at the age of 9 and my first elk at the age of 12. I taught my two boys to shoot and, like most families in my area, I took them hunting. Whenever my grandkids come to visit you can bet there is a lot of shooting going on at my place. That is my reality, and that's how I was raised, how I raised my children, and how my grandchildren are being raised.

Charlie Culp practicing archery.

It is gratifying to see a young person learn to shoot and learn gun safety and the responsibilities of using a gun. By the way, none of my guns have ever "assaulted" anyone.

My granddaughter Charlie is eight years old and can out-shoot some adults with a gun and a bow and arrow. "Aim small, miss small," Charlie!

In Republic, almost every household has at least one gun in it, most have several, and others have what could be considered an "arsenal." Guns are a part of our lives, and we use them often. We grew up with them and were taught the responsibilities that come along with being a gun owner. We hunt with them. We protect ourselves, our animals (both livestock and pets) and our property with them. This is a way of life for us. It is a shared belief that guns in the hands of good people stop bad people from doing bad things. Guns are used every day in this country for self-defense, target practice, and hunting. Where I live and work, guns are an integral part of life.

> *"To preserve liberty, it is essential that the whole body of people always possess arms, and be taught alike especially when young, how to use them."*
> *– Richard Henry Lee*

The response from my post was very positive. Most of the time I'll get a few likes or comments. Sometimes I manage to get over one hundred, but that usually only happens if it includes a picture and story of my excellent K9 partner Karma (back cover) or my former K9 Isko.

The first post I made about I1639, on November 7, 2018, the day after the vote, received over 400 comments and over 3.5K likes, hearts or smiley faces. It has been shared 2,366 times to date. In addition to all the positive responses on Facebook, I received the same positive in-person responses from my fellow citizens.

One has to wonder with the Facebook algorithms continually changing, and the generally small number of actual views any post might get on any given day, how is it that this one gained so much attention? Why was it so much more popular than any other posts I've done? All I was doing was stating the fact that all police officers learn in the police academy; don't violate anyone's rights.

We know what happens when someone's rights are violated. More often than not, the violator, department, and city are sued in court. Not only that but if you do violate someone's rights you have made them a victim—a victim of an oppressive police officer. That is what the vast majority of us have sworn an oath not to do. You could lose everything that you have worked for including your career and your freedom.

"The supreme power in America cannot enforce unjust laws by the sword, because the whole body of the people are armed, and constitute a force superior to any band of regular troops." – Noah Webster

To follow up that post, on November 9th, I decided that I would recommend an ordinance to the City Council that would ensure the City Police would never violate someone's gun rights, even long after I retire. I used verbiage I found from the 10th Amendment Center and old city ordinances to create what I thought was needed—a "Second Amendment Sanctuary City" ordinance.

I emailed it to the city council members and the mayor for their consideration. I also posted it on the Facebook page asking citizens what they thought. Here is what that post said, including the proposed ordinance (Note: you can still visit this post on our Facebook page: Friends of Republic Police WA and see it there):

"I can't make legislation, but I can recommend it, which I have. What do you think?"

Ordinance Number: _____

An ORDINANCE of the City of Republic, which shall be known and may be cited as the "2nd Amendment

Sanctuary City Ordinance." To prevent federal and state infringement on the right to keep and bear arms; nullifying all federal and state acts in violation of the 2nd Amendment to the Constitution of the United States and Article 1 Section 24 of the Washington State Constitution.

WHEREAS, the City of Republic believes that:

A. The 2nd Amendment to the Constitution of the United States reads as follows, "A well-regulated militia, being necessary to the security of a free state, the right of the people to keep and bear arms shall not be infringed."

B. Article 1 Section 24 of the Washington State Constitution reads as follows, "The right of the individual citizen to bear arms in defense of himself, or the state, shall not be impaired, but nothing in this section shall be construed as authorizing individuals or corporations to organize, maintain or employ an armed body of men."

C. All federal and State acts, laws, orders, rules or regulations regarding firearms, firearm accessories, and ammunition are a violation of the 2nd Amendment to the U.S. Constitution and Article 1 Section 24 of the Washington State Constitution.

NOW, THEREFORE, THE CITY COUNCIL OF THE CITY OF REPUBLIC, WASHINGTON STATE, DO ORDAIN AS FOLLOWS:

SECTION 1: PROHIBITION ON STATE AND FEDERAL INFRINGEMENT OF THE RIGHT TO KEEP AND BEAR ARMS

A. The Republic City Council declares that all federal and state acts, laws, orders, rules and regulations past, present or future, in violation of the U.S. and/ or State Constitutions are not authorized by the said Constitutions and violate the true meaning and intent as given by the Founders and Ratifiers and are hereby declared to be invalid in the City of Republic, shall not be recognized by the City of Republic, are specifically rejected by the City of Republic and shall be considered null and void and of no effect in the City of Republic.

B. No agent, employee, or official of the City of Republic, or any corporation providing services to the City of Republic shall provide material support or participate in any way with the implementation of federal or state acts, orders, rules, laws or regulations in violation of the 2nd Amendment to the United States Constitution and Article 1 Section 24 of the Washington State Constitution.

C. Nothing in this Ordinance shall affect City Ordinance 94-05 which prohibits, for safety reasons, the discharge of firearms in the City limits except in the defense of self or others.

SECTION 2: REQUESTED INVOLVEMENT OF NEIGHBORING COMMUNITIES

The City of Republic calls upon other local jurisdictions within the State of Washington to join us in this action by passing a similar ordinance.

SECTION 3: URGING ACTION BY THE STATE GOVERNMENT

The City of Republic requests that copies of this ordinance be immediately transmitted to each individual legislator that represents our district in the State government urging each to introduce similar legislation on a state level during the next legislative session.

SECTION 4: SEVERABILITY CLAUSE

If any provisions of this ordinance or its application to any person or circumstance are held invalid, the remainder of the Ordinance or the application of the provision to other persons or circumstances is not affected.

SECTION 5: EFFECTIVE DATE

This Ordinance shall become effective from and after the date of its passage by the City Council, approval by the Mayor and five (5) days after publication as required by law.

This post was very active with over 300 comments and 1.3K likes and over 900 shares. What happened next was unexpected! The phones started ringing, and the emails started flowing in. I don't mean just a few. I mean hundreds of emails, phone calls, and letters were delivered to the city. The dispatch center, which is part of the Ferry County Sheriff's Office, was also getting calls.

The vast majority of correspondence was positive and supported what I had proposed. I was getting so many emails and calls that I couldn't keep up (even though I tried!).

However, as you can guess, not all the correspondence was positive. There were some who called for me to be fired. I had messages that said I needed to 'shut up and sit down' and some that said my job is to 'enforce the law and I either needed to do that or resign.' When I became a police officer, it was because I believed I could make a difference. I believe in what I do. Also, there is no way I can violate my oath to uphold the Constitution in good conscience.

My stance on NOT violating someone's constitutional rights started hitting our "local" news stations in Spokane (3 hours away) and the local papers. The main point I think that caught everyone's attention was "Sanctuary City." It had been used regularly in regards to Sanctuary Cities and States who won't uphold the laws of the United States when it comes to illegal immigrants. Using it for a constitutional right only seemed fitting to me and a very appropriate use of the term in the current political climate. After all, illegal border crossing is a crime but owning a gun is a right. Why not have a sanctuary for our rights that are obviously under attack? The entire United States should be a sanctuary for our rights; that is what our founders wrote, and that is the law of the land.

As of the writing of this book, I have no idea what the City Council will do with my proposal. Regardless of whether they adopt it or not, that is entirely up to them and the people they represent. It is well within their job description to do either. No matter the outcome my position remains the same when it comes to law enforcement and protection in the City of Republic.

I will do the right thing no matter what they decide; I will not violate citizens' rights and neither will any officer who works under me. If they do nothing, then I can't help but wonder what or who will protect the rights of the citizens when I leave here.

Chapter 4

NATIONAL MEDIA COMES TO TOWN

"It is increasingly important to be open-minded."
– Tucker Carlson

Following my viral post, the Fox News Channel sent Dan Springer, along with a camera crew, to report on our story in Republic. While in town, they interviewed me as well as Mayor Koontz. They were in town for a couple of days taking video of our small town and completing their assignment to cover the "Sanctuary City" story. Little Republic, WA, was now in the spotlight, and people across the nation heard about my stance on prime-time TV. After that aired, I was invited on the Fox News Channel to appear live via Skype on the Fox and Friends Sunday show. They wanted a more in-depth interview about what I was doing and what the City Council was going to do concerning Initiative 1639.

I am good at handling and training dogs, doing criminal investigations and helping people by putting criminals in jail. That's what I do most often and what I know how to do well. I have never given a news conference; I've never had a need to, let alone been live on a national news show!

Please note, I am not a good public speaker, and I'll be the first to admit that. To say I was nervous is an understatement! I've been told there is no growth without some pain. I felt that this issue and the flagrant violation of rights it employed were worth the pain, so I agreed to do the show. I have never been comfortable standing in front of a crowd and speaking, but I also understood that the time to speak up was now and the opportunity I had been given was not to be taken for granted. Someone had to do it and apparently that someone was going to be me.

I have worked closely over the years with Ferry County Sheriff Sergeant Talon Venturo. Talon is a 'go-getter' and a great public speaker. Talon and I have done many criminal cases together, mostly involving narcotics and burglaries. Although our area has a small population, we have both testified in Federal Court and put people away for decades because of what they have done.

We have a motto that we say whenever we are about to execute a search warrant or work an informant: "let's do what we do." We both have it tattooed on our arms. This was my time to do what I do, and although I had doubts that I was up for the challenge, I remembered our motto and did it anyway.

Just before the show, a professional from Fox assured me it was no big deal, only 2.5 million viewers were watching. Two and a half MILLION? I don't even like a crowd of 2.5 let alone in the millions. However, as they say in showbiz, the show must go on!

I slept for maybe an hour the night before. What if I can't talk? What if I forget what to say or can't answer a question? These thoughts circled in my head and wouldn't allow me a minute to rest. Friends messaged me with advice; don't say "uh," don't chew gum, and don't embarrass us. Ok, no pressure, nope, none at all! Just another day at the office, right? My doubts about my capabilities talking on national TV ran through my head like a mouse on a wheel. Nonetheless, I had made a commitment, and that was the way it was going to be.

The producer from FOX called on the phone and then on Skype. Before I went on live TV in front of all these people, a technician did a video, lighting and sound check. They had to make sure that the lighting was excellent and we could hear each other! The funny thing about this interview though is that I could not see them, but they could see me. I was looking at a blank computer screen. They told me to look right into the camera. Ok. I stare into the little round thing on top of the screen. Got it.

I don't know about you, but I sweat a lot when I'm nervous. I can still function and think clearly when I'm nervous and that's good for police work, but sweating and being all shiny on TV doesn't look good. Now my wife, bless her heart, keeps the house a little too hot for my comfort, so just before we went on air I opened all the windows and put a fan behind the computer blowing air directly on me. It was in the low 30's outside, so my wife chose to be in another room. No shine here, lights, camera, action…makeup?

I had several things I wanted to say, and I had put a few reminders on post-it notes around my computer so I wouldn't forget. I had no idea what kind of questions I would be asked from the hosts of the show. I was told I would be on air around 5-7 minutes. That seemed like a very long time to me! What was I expected to talk about for that amount of time? After all, I was just a cop saying I wouldn't violate people's rights.

I didn't ask for this. I wondered why this was happening to me. All kinds of thoughts were racing through my head: don't forget to say this, don't forget to mention that, and don't say "uh"! I heard someone say "30 seconds, right when we come back from break you're on." Ok, here we go, I thought to myself: "let's do what we do." You are either going to embarrass everyone in Republic or make them proud on national TV. A quick sip of water and it was time…and then it was over.

I couldn't believe how quickly the time passed. It seemed like it was over within 30 seconds! I remember telling my wife afterward that they cut it short for some reason, I didn't even get to say much! It was only after watching it on TV that I realized I had been on for over 5 minutes. Time really does fly when you are having fun…or something like that. The response from viewers all across the nation was 99% positive. I even got emails of support from Australia and England!

I later appeared again on the Fox News Channel on The Tucker Carlson Tonight show. I have watched Tucker for years, and I am a big fan. By the time I did his show I had already interviewed with dozens of TV and radio shows and had become a little more comfortable on camera. It turned out fine because Tucker is a great host and I was getting better at it with each new interview.

The next day after the Fox and Friends interview was the scheduled City Council meeting. Because of the enormous amount of interest, the mayor moved the meeting to the school multi-purpose room instead of the small room the meetings are generally held in. At a typical council meeting, there might be five people, rarely over ten. For this meeting over 200 people showed up! The media was there with a camera crew as well as an internet-based news reporter from the Center for Self-Governance. My stance on Initiative 1639 was garnering a lot more attention than I was prepared for!

Mayor Elbert Koontz called the meeting to order and we all stood for the flag salute. Then the mayor called me up to speak. As usual, I was nervous, but I knew the time was upon me to stand up for what I believed.

Whether I wanted to be a part of it or not, I was, and it was time to stand up for people's right to bear arms again. I walked up to the microphone and began to speak.

The microphone didn't work! No one could hear me past the third row, and there were lots of rows! A million thoughts went through my head. What do I do now? Start hollering so everyone can hear me? This is embarrassing. Everyone is looking at me! Are we live on TV right now? This can't be happening.

I looked up at Mayor Koontz for help, and, like a lighthouse in a storm, he was holding a spare microphone. The time came, and I began my speech. The sweat was rolling off my head and "let's do what we do" was a constant mantra in my mind. This is the speech I gave that night:

> *"After Initiative 1639 passed, I had a citizen who was concerned that law enforcement in Republic was going to start arresting people under 21 for having semi-auto rifles. After all, guns are an integral part of life here and many places across our nation. God, guns, and guts are what made this country. So they were rightly concerned.*
>
> *I assured them that that would be a violation of their constitutional rights and we would not be doing that here. After several people came up to me with the same concern, I felt the need to get the word out to everyone in Republic, so I posted just that on Facebook. I also*

wrote up a proposal for a city ordinance which all of the Council has received.

I never dreamed that a police officer stating that he will NOT violate anyone's constitutional rights would be such a big deal. That's police work 101 — don't violate anyone's rights! If the voters in this state passed an initiative saying that the police can violate any of the other constitutional rights, I would feel the same way, and I would not violate those rights either. If an officer does violate someone's rights, it's all over the news showing the police as oppressive. Now, I've said I wouldn't violate anyone's rights, and it's all over the news too. Weird.

This initiative is wrong, not just for the words written in it, but for the entire process, and here's why:

We are a nation founded on the rule of law, and the basis for all law is the Constitution. The rule of law is what our founders set up in our Republic. Notice I said Republic and not democracy. Our town is named with a word that has a very special meaning. You can search our nation's founding documents from beginning to end and nowhere in the founding documents of our nation will you find the word democracy. Our founders hated democracy.

The Constitution guarantees to each state a republican form of government. That is written in the Constitution; democracy is not. Our founders set us up as a republic which is the rule of law.

In a democracy it is majority rule. That is what is being practiced right now in Washington State — democracy. In a Republic the minority is protected by law and those laws can only be changed by the peoples' representatives, not by a popular vote and the laws cannot go against the Constitution. In a democracy the majority rules over the minority and in this case the big cities are telling us what is allowed and what isn't. It's like three wolves and one sheep voting on what's for dinner.

If you do a simple google search, you will find the founding fathers speaking against the evils of democracy. The majority is often wrong, and in this case, they are for sure. Our founders were some pretty smart people.

Our State Constitution says, "The right of the individual citizen to bear arms in defense of himself, or the state, shall not be impaired." This initiative impairs individual citizens' rights not only protected by Section 24 of the State Constitution but the 2nd and 4th Amendments to the U.S. Constitution as well. It requires people to turn over their medical records for government inspection and requires payment to the State in order to exercise your rights. It also makes criminals out of otherwise law-abiding citizens.

The Bill of Rights are instructions for the limitations on the government, not the governed. Some people have told me that I should wait for the courts to decide. Although I do not doubt that the Supreme

Court will rule against this initiative when it gets to them, I feel it is my duty to uphold my oath of office not to violate anyone's rights and so I won't.

I have only submitted a draft proposal to the Council. I know that there has to be time for you all to review and digest it and most likely have the City attorney look it over before it is even brought up for a vote.

I do not expect, and no one here should expect, a vote on this tonight. That is not how the process works on any ordinance. I hope that the City Council will do their due diligence as they always have before. We have some great leaders on the City Council and as mayor. All of them have told me that they are strong supporters of our constitutional rights including the right to bear arms.

In closing, I did not ask for all of the attention that my position has brought, and it is a shame that a police officer standing up for citizens' rights is an anomaly. Our elected leaders can't make America Great Again by themselves; it will take every one of us doing our part.

I will stand up for citizens' rights, and I won't back down. Thank you."

As soon as I finished speaking, everyone stood up and clapped and cheered! The citizens' reaction melted all the stress, and it touched me deeply. I felt the love and support like I have never felt before. There was no doubt left, if there was any to begin with, that I was doing the right thing for my community.

After that speech, I was interviewed by a Spokane TV reporter, Kyle Simchuck. Kyle drove six hours round trip from Spokane, over the highest open mountain pass in the state to be there and get the story for the news. I also did an interview on Facebook Live with Mark from the Center for Self-Governance, an organization that teaches people about the government and their rights.

While everyone was leaving the meeting, I stood in the hallway. I received a lot of hugs and handshakes from the people I serve. It was an amazing night and reaffirmed my belief that I was doing the right thing. I knew then that the people I worked for had my back and understood what and why I was doing what I was doing.

Recordings of my speech, the interviews, and the reaction afterward are posted on November 19th, 2018 on my Facebook page, Friends of Republic Police WA.

I had several more interviews with the media in the days that followed, including Tucker Carlson, as I have already mentioned, and Dana Loesch with NRA TV, and many other news organizations all across the country. From Texas to Boston to Seattle word got around that someone was taking a stand for people's right to bear arms and a massive amount of the people appreciated it! One interview lasted for an hour on a talk radio show from Boston. Emails and calls kept pouring in. People in the area showed their support for my ordinance by making shirts and buttons that said, "We the People Stand with Chief Culp" and "We've got your 6 Chief Culp."

Since then I've gotten more comfortable with interviews and, as of this writing, mid-January 2019, I am still doing

them quite regularly. I'll admit they have gotten more natural to do. Experience is a good teacher.

I never asked to be in the spotlight, and I know this isn't about me. It's about our God-given rights. It's about our way of life. It's about standing up for and protecting the rights of all people across our

Republic residents Keith and Chris Robins showing support.

great nation. That stand is what garnered all of this attention in the first place, and I'll gladly stand up for our constitutional rights anywhere and everywhere, at any time, no matter how uncomfortable I might feel!

Chapter 5

RULE OF LAW OR MAJORITY RULE?

"A Republic if you can keep it."
– Benjamin Franklin

What we see in Washington State with the initiative process is exactly what our founding fathers warned us about over 200 years ago: direct democracy, which is majority rule. Oh but wait, we are a democracy aren't we? If everyone says we are, including presidents of the United States and the people we watch on the nightly news, it has to be correct, right?

Many people believe that the United States is a democracy, but I've got news for you, and again I encourage you to keep an open mind. What I have to say may have you second guessing if what you have been taught your whole life is correct. Let me explain.

Democracy is majority rule. A lynch mob is an example of majority rule. If a group of people says you stole a horse and decided your punishment is hanging, you are the victim of democracy/mob rule. Democracy is when the majority tramples on the rights of the minority. That's it in a nutshell. The majority rules in a democracy, and the minority does not have a voice and mostly has to go along with whatever the majority wants.

Our great country was set up to protect everyone's rights. Regardless of what the majority of people think yesterday, today or tomorrow, your inalienable rights are always protected by the rule of law, the Constitution.

I remember the term 'democracy' being pounded into my head when I was in school back in the 1970s. "Majority rules" was repeated by teachers constantly. Being taught that "The United States is a democracy," was and still is in the curriculum. Today this myth is perpetuated on credible police training websites such as the Washington State Criminal Justice Training Commission, where it says: "Training the Guardians of Democracy." However, just because it is still being taught, even by credible institutions, does not mean it is true. I've heard that if you repeat a lie often enough, people will believe it, but that doesn't make it a fact.

If we don't have a democracy then what did our founders give us and why does it even matter? Let's explore this together.

Just after the Constitutional Convention in 1787, Benjamin Franklin was asked what form of government they had given us. His reply was, "A Republic if you can keep it." Our founding fathers did give us a republic, not a democracy. So many times our political leaders and the media mistakenly refer to our government as a democracy, which is not true. Those who are saying this are either misinformed, blind followers of others, or doing the unthinkable — intentionally misleading the masses. A republic and a democracy are not the same. They are opposites. Here's why.

A republican form of government is "rule by law." That law is the Constitution here in the United States. A democracy is a rule by the majority, which enables a "mob rule" mentality and soon leads to anarchy and chaos. If the majority decides what will be, the minority becomes oppressed.

However, don't just take my word for it, our founders knew the dangers of democracy from studying nations of the world throughout its history. Let's see what they had to say about this subject:

Some founders quotes:

> *George Washington, "...the preservation...of the republican model of government."*
>
> *Virginia's Edmund Randolph, "...to provide a cure for the evils under which the United States labored; that*

in tracing these evils to their origin every man had found it in the turbulence and trials of democracy..."

Samuel Adams, "Democracy never lasts long. It soon wastes, exhausts and murders itself. There was never a democracy that 'did not commit suicide.'"

Alexander Hamilton, "It has been observed that a pure democracy, if it were practicable, would be the most perfect government. Experience has proved that no position is more false than this. The ancient democracies, in which the people themselves deliberated, never possessed one good feature of government. Their very character was tyranny; their figure deformity. We are a Republican Government. Real liberty is never found in despotism or in the extremes of Democracy."

Fisher Ames, "Democracy, in its best state, is but the politics of Bedlam; while kept chained, its thoughts are frantic, but when it breaks loose, it kills the keeper, fires the building, and perishes." In an essay entitled "The Mire of Democracy," he wrote that the framers of the Constitution "intended our government should be a republic, which differs more widely from a democracy than a democracy from a despotism."

James Madison, "...democracies have ever been spectacles of turbulence and contention, have ever been found incompatible with personal security, or the rights of property, and have in general been as short in their lives as they are violent in their deaths."

How long has it been since you said the Pledge of Allegiance? When we say the Pledge to the flag, it is "to the Republic for which it stands," not to the democracy for which it stands:

"I pledge allegiance to the flag of the United States of America and to the REPUBLIC for which it stands, one nation, under God, indivisible, with liberty and justice for all."

You can search the founding documents from beginning to end, top to bottom, front to back and you will not find the word democracy referenced anywhere. It's not even mentioned. Not once! It is clear that we are NOT a democracy.

The founding fathers never set us up as one, and they never intended us to be one! It is obvious to me, our founders hated democracy. They studied history and knew the dangers of the public and a majority vote when it came to making laws. The good news is we are guaranteed a republican form of government. It is written in our foundational document, the U.S. Constitution, just for that reason. They knew what they were doing, and they certainly felt it was important enough to include it in black and white:

U.S. Constitution Article 4 Section 4

The United States shall guarantee to every State in this Union a Republican Form of Government and shall protect each of them against Invasion, and on

Application of the Legislature, or of the Executive (when the Legislature cannot be convened) against domestic violence.

I am not writing this book to point fingers and delve into the reasons why some people have attempted to change our form of government by repeating the lie that we are a democracy in newsprint, on TV, or the internet or why some have misled others through incorrect educational practices to believe what is just not true. I don't have any idea what their motives may be, but I will point out that several notable people loved democracy. I'll let them speak for themselves.

Karl Marx, in his book The Communist Manifesto: "... the first step in the revolution by the working class is to raise the proletariat to the position of ruling class, to win the battle of democracy...abolish private property... wrest, by degrees, capital from the bourgeoisie... centralize all instruments of production in the hands of the State."

Chinese Communist Leader Mao Tse-tung, "Taken as a whole, the Chinese revolutionary movement led by the Communist Party embraces the two stages, i.e., the democratic and the socialist revolutions, which are essentially different revolutionary processes, and the second process can be carried through only after the first has been completed. The democratic revolution is the necessary preparation for the socialist revolution, and the socialist revolution is the inevitable sequel to the democratic revolution. The ultimate aim for which all communists strive is to bring about a socialist and communist society."

Russian President Mikhail Gorbachev, who stated in his 1987 book Perestroika that, "According to Lenin, socialism and democracy are indivisible...The essence of perestroika lies in the fact that it unites socialism with democracy and revives the Leninist concept...We want more socialism and, therefore, more democracy." (Reference: "The New American Magazine" November 6, 2000)

It is a hard pill to swallow when you see the most notorious leaders in history talking favorably about democracy as a way to strategically take over society. So why would anyone want to believe that the United States is a democracy? Ignorance is not bliss. It's incredible to me how few people in our country genuinely understand the republican form of government we have been given and how little respect we give it. As Benjamin Franklin said, "We have a Republic, if you can keep it." Now that you have this accurate historical information, you don't have to mistakenly believe or say that the United States is a democracy. It's not.

Chapter 6

OUR RIGHTS AND RESPONSIBILITIES

"[T]he moment that idea is admitted into society, that property is not as sacred as the Laws of God, and that there is not a force of law and public justice to protect it, anarchy and tyranny commence. Property must be sacred, or liberty cannot exist." – John Adams

Have you ever asked yourself where our rights come from? Some people say we get our rights from the Bill of Rights. Our liberty and rights are not something given to us by a document, the courts, or our elected officials in any branch of government. Our Constitution doesn't give us our rights nor does The Bill of Rights.

Our rights are God-given, we are "endowed by our Creator" with them. We are born with them. All the power the government has in the United States of

America was given to it by the citizens. Those powers are limited, defined and enumerated in our founding documents: The Constitution and the Bill of Rights. The Declaration of Independence says:

> *"We hold these truths to be self-evident, that all men are created equal, that their Creator endows them with certain Unalienable Rights, that among these are Life, Liberty and the pursuit of Happiness. — That to secure these rights, Governments are instituted among Men, deriving their just powers from the consent of the governed."*

Our founders knew the importance of our rights. They were not giving them to us by creating the best country the world has ever known. Instead, they were protecting those rights through our founding documents; "That to secure these rights, Governments are instituted…" The men who set up our country understood the dangers of direct democracy. They understood the dangers of the majority.

That is why they set up the Electoral College for presidential elections, not the popular vote. That is also the reason they had the State legislators pick U.S. senators originally. They gave us a constitutional republic, ruled by law. A representative form of government, not by the majority but by elected officials representing the people. This should be crystal clear now if it wasn't before.

In Washington State, initially, the legislature alone was empowered to make laws as our founding fathers intended, not by a vote of the people. That was changed in the early 1900s. The initiative process has been used to limit freedom ever since. It has also been used to limit vehicle taxes, but we all know how that has worked out; the state government keeps raising the vehicle tax anyway. Swaying public opinion is easy if you have enough money and if the public does not take the initiative to stay informed. Here is one example for you:

If you have never seen the movie "Where the Red Fern Grows" I encourage you to watch it with your family or read the book by the same name. It is a terrific family story about a boy and his hunting dogs 'Ann' and 'Dan.' The boy worked hard, saved his own money and bought two puppies that he trained to hunt. He had many adventures with his two hound buddies.

When I was growing up, we had hunting dogs. When my kids were young we had hunting dogs too; Candy, Goober, Spotty, Reba and Blitz were some of the names of dogs we had through the years. Most of them we raised from puppies, and our whole family loved them.

My wife and I spent many weekends camping with our boys and dogs in and around the Olympic Peninsula, in the northwestern part of Washington, hunting and enjoying our time as a young family.

Hunting with hounds is a perfect way to control the predator population. Cougars and bobcats eat a lot of deer, elk and small game, such as grouse and rabbits. Thinning the predators through hunting helps the other animals and is good wildlife management to keep the predator and prey population in balance. It is also an excellent way to see a bear, cougar or bobcat up close with or without shooting it.

Many times the dogs would get an animal up a tree, and we would take pictures of it. Believe it or not, sometimes I would even climb up in the tree with a wild cat and take close up pictures! After that, we would leash the dogs and walk back to the truck leaving the animal alive, taking only memories of being out in the mountains with our family and dogs. Many times we took our boys' friends with us, too. This is one of the

Loren in a tree with a wild bobcat.

only ways for kids to see a mountain lion up close and in the wild. We had many good times together.

Professionals set the hunting seasons at the Department of Wildlife. Based on science, wildlife managers set seasons and bag limits to optimize the resource. The reason I'm telling you about this part of my life is that an initiative of the people—democracy in action/mob rule—took that away from us.

We had to stop hunting with our dogs, as did many families across our state. Not because it was based on science or sound wildlife management to do so, because it wasn't. This decision was based solely on emotion. Organizations like the Humane Society of the United

Up close and personal with a mountain lion.

States pushed to outlaw hunting with dogs for specific game animals. With millions of dollars and preying on the pure emotion of the people, they could advertise an initiative to the people to outlaw what many families like mine have done for generations.

My grandfather hunted with dogs. My dad hunted with dogs as he was growing up. I hunted with my dad and our dogs, and when I had my boys, we continued this family tradition. Sadly, I will never get to have that experience with my grandchildren. It is a hunting tradition and method that is as old as the first person who ever domesticated a wolf.

Because the majority of voters, most of whom have probably never set foot in the outdoors to hunt their own food, decided that they didn't want anyone to hunt certain animals with dogs, an initiative was passed. The average voter knows nothing about wildlife management or game populations, and yet they decided that we shouldn't hunt with dogs because it looked cruel. So they banned it.

But let me ask you this: have you stopped to realize that burger, steak or hotdog you eat was killed before being cut up for your BBQ? It isn't pretty to watch a cow or a pig get shot in the head or a chicken having its head cut off before it becomes food on the table. But something has to die for you to eat.

Some people say that's not true because they don't eat meat and therefore don't kill animals. Animals die so people can have tofu, carrots, lettuce, and potatoes. If you think the farmer who grows your food is going to let rabbits, grasshoppers, worms, deer, and gophers eat his profit, then you are mistaken. What farmer in their right mind would try to make a living selling crops, only to allow wildlife to eat the harvest before he could sell it?

Whatever gets in the way between that farmer and his profit is either poisoned, trapped, shot or run over by a tractor. That is the cruel reality! However, because people go to the grocery store and buy nice clean groceries (including meat), they get to ignore the facts of what had to die so they could eat. To some, it seems barbaric when they see videos of people who are hands-on and kill their own food.

That is what the proponents of eliminating our type of hunting did. They showed videos on TV of animals being killed and they swayed public opinion. That's the danger of democracy! The public can be influenced by whoever has the most money to do it. Why did they ban hunting certain animals with dogs and not all hunting? Because a minority of people hunt with dogs, so it was easy to get the majority to go along with it. Many people, even other hunters, did not stop this because it didn't affect them.

This is just another example of liberties being taken from the minority by the majority. That is democracy in action. That is the initiative process. If you have enough money and can convince enough people, then you can get anything passed. Direct democracy means everything is up for grabs based on the will of the majority. The minority, well, sorry, suck it up.

> *"Guard against the impostures of pretended patriotism." – George Washington*

> *"The truth is, all might be free if they valued freedom, and defended it as they ought." – Samuel Adams*

How can we as a people agree what is and isn't constitutional if we can't accept that the Constitution is the most significant founding document for any country and that it is THE supreme law of our land? Because in a world where the Constitution doesn't matter, anything goes and go they will! Your rights, my rights, everybody's rights, right out the window!

If we don't hold our government within the boundaries of this document and the rules that it enumerates, then how can we complain when we lose our God-given rights?

How can anyone, in one breath, say it's ok to infringe on the rights of others, even though those things are guaranteed secure by the Constitution, and then in the next breath say "but don't you dare touch my freedom of speech or my right to peacefully assemble?"

Is one part of this document different than another to be picked apart at the whim of a politician or the will of the masses? If it's not written correctly, or it needs to be changed, then change it! It describes precisely how to do that, but don't stand by and let people walk on it while it's still the law of the land!

I will agree and hold this to be a solid truth: if it's not written in the Constitution as something our government has the responsibility to do, then it's left for the "States and or the People," according to the Tenth Amendment. If it IS written that a right "Shall not be infringed" then it shall not! A simple truth but an important one.

If we allow the Constitution to be bent, then we have no defense when it comes time for the will of the government or the majority of voters to take our guns, our land, our money, our freedom, and our liberties. After all, we allowed the Constitution to be bent before when it suited us or didn't affect us individually. Once that's done it's hard to stop the obvious usurpations that follow. Who will be there to defend you then?

Our Constitution was set up to be the backbone of our republic. Our rights and liberties are too important to be left to the ever-changing prevailing winds of politicians or the shifting sands of public opinion in an initiative. Our founders knew this when they made our Constitution difficult to change. They knew this when they refused to make our country a democracy.

"Precedents are dangerous things. Let the reins of government then be braced and held with a steady

hand, and every violation of the Constitution be reprehended. If defective, let it be amended, but not suffered to be trampled upon while it has an existence." – George Washington

Have you ever taken an oath to uphold and defend the Constitution? Are you bound by one now? Before joining the military or becoming a police officer anywhere in the United States or taking office (in the case of a county sheriff or other elected official), an oath is administered and sworn to.

Most police officers and deputies are well aware of the 4th and 5th Amendments because we deal with those all the time when we read Miranda warnings to a suspect or apply for a search warrant. I wonder if many have read the rest of it. Don't we take an oath to uphold and

Loren official U.S. Army photo 1980.

defend the Constitution, all of it? Why do we take that oath and where did it come from; who said we have to do that? If you are a police officer or sheriff, do you remember what you said when you made that solemn promise?

I remember when I joined the Army back in 1980. I was so proud when I raised my hand to swear the oath. At nineteen I didn't know what it meant "to uphold and defend the Constitution," but I do now.

For those of you, like me, who didn't know what it meant: you said you promised. You gave your word to uphold and defend the Constitution of the United States and the Constitution of your respective state. That's what elected officials, the military and the police swear to, but why?

That oath is not required because someone in your department thought it would be a good idea or your city council or county commissioners came up with it one day. We take that oath because of our founding fathers. They thought it was of great importance that a person gives their word before taking office in government.

This was so important that they wrote it in as part of our Constitution. We take the oath because our founding fathers made it the law when they founded our country. That's how important a man's word was during the birth of our nation.

U.S. Constitution Article 6

3: The Senators and Representatives before mentioned, and the Members of the several State Legislatures, and all executive and judicial Officers, both of the United States and of the several States, shall be bound by Oath or Affirmation, to support this Constitution; but no religious Test shall ever be required as a Qualification to any Office or public Trust under the United States.

Let's break it down a bit. "ALL Executive Officers," police are a part of the executive branch. Remember there are three branches of government: Executive, Judicial and Legislative. "Both of the United States and of the several States…" So not only Federal officials but officials in the states as well. "Shall be BOUND by Oath or Affirmation to support this Constitution."

These are words written into the Constitution by our founding fathers well over 200 years ago. How do you think they felt about taking an oath? This was not something they took lightly.

These men put their lives and fortunes on the line. They were committing what was considered treason against the world's superpower at the time, and it was a crime punishable by death. Of course, their word meant something!

Their word was as solid as their handshake. I remember a time when a handshake meant something. It was everything for someone to keep an oath. Our founding fathers didn't include it lightly when they wrote it in our founding document as a requirement for officers at the federal and state level.

These were times when, if a man was insulted, he challenged the insulter to a duel. They went out back, walked off thirty paces, then turned around and shot at each other, often leading to the death of one or both. These people were serious about duty, honor, country and their word meant something!

The part of the State Constitution in Washington State that relates to guns, Article 1 Section 24, is very clear when it says:

"The right of the individual citizen to bear arms in defense of himself, or the state, shall not be impaired, but nothing in this section shall be construed as authorizing individuals or corporations to organize, maintain or employ an armed body of men."

There have been arguments about the Second Amendment to the Federal Constitution mostly concerning the word "Militia." It has been settled to a great extent by the U.S. Supreme Court when they decreed it is an INDIVIDUAL right. District of Columbia v Heller rightfully said that it is a right for the individual, unconnected to service in the Militia.

"The best we can hope for concerning the people at large is that they be properly armed." – Alexander Hamilton

The Washington State Constitution doesn't even have the word Militia in it.

"The right of the individual citizen." That would be pretty much everyone who is a citizen. "Bear arms." Bear means I have them; I'm carrying them. "Defense of himself or the state" means I can shoot someone if I need to defend myself or the state. That right is crystal clear, so let's move on because it gets better!

If you don't live in Washington State, bear with me for a bit and then see what your state Constitution says because I bet it is something similar to this:

Washington State Constitution:

Article 1 SECTION 2

SUPREME LAW OF THE LAND. "The Constitution of the United States is the supreme law of the land."

What did that say? You read it right. The Constitution is the "SUPREME LAW" of the LAND. Keeping this focused in on the subject we are dealing with here in Washington State and many other states, guns, this means that a law contrary to the Second Amendment is no law at all because the Constitution IS the SUPREME LAW.

Article 1 SECTION 6

OATHS - MODE OF ADMINISTERING. "The mode of administering an oath, or affirmation, shall be such as may be most consistent with and binding upon the conscience of the person to whom such oath, or affirmation, may be administered."

Article 1 SECTION 29

CONSTITUTION MANDATORY. "The provisions of this Constitution are mandatory unless by express words they are declared to be otherwise."

So, not only did the founders include oaths in the U.S. Constitution but the founders of Washington State felt it necessary to add it as well. Government officials are expected to swear an oath that is "binding upon the conscience of the person" and the "provisions of this Constitution are mandatory." How anyone can expect someone, who took an oath and understands what it means, to disregard that oath and enforce anything that violates the Constitution is beyond comprehension to me! I feel that when you take an oath, you do so with the expectation of keeping that oath. There can be no other way!

Chapter 7

KEEPING THE PEACE

"But I'm in Law Enforcement. It's my job to enforce the law!" – Misinformed Cop

"The essence of tyranny is the enforcement of stupid laws." – Edmund Burke

I've heard the above "Misinformed Cop" quote from far too many police leaders recently. Since I believe it's wrong to enforce an unconstitutional initiative, it makes me cringe when I hear cops say they have to enforce a law simply "because it's the law." Police chiefs and sheriffs who use that reasoning also need to remember their sworn oath to "defend." I want to ask several questions to those in police work and discuss "enforcing laws" versus defending the public's rights.

Would you enforce a law that says people of a particular color cannot use certain water fountains or ride in the front of a bus? Would you be the officer to arrest Rosa Parks because it was the law and you were law enforcement? On December 1st, 1955, Rosa Parks boarded a bus and sat in the black-only section. When white people boarded the bus, the driver told some black people, including Rosa, to move toward the back and give up their seats to the white people. Rosa refused to move. The bus driver called the police, and she was arrested. In her book, Parks wrote that she didn't move because she was physically tired, but because she was tired of giving in. When she asked why she was being pushed around, the police officer said, "I don't know, but the law is the law, and you are under arrest." Saying you have to uphold the law because you are a law enforcement officer is a cop out, pun intended!

If a law violates the Constitution, which, remember, is "the supreme law" of the land, then we have no obligation to enforce it; it would be against your oath of office if you did. In Nazi Germany, they blindly followed "the law" when they exterminated millions of Jews. Would you do that because "it's the law"? I would hope not! How did that defense work at the Nuremberg trials?

A Washington state police officer who says he has to enforce the law because he is a "law enforcement officer" should review his certification paperwork given to him by the State when he graduated from the police academy. Washington State doesn't certify Law Enforcement Officers, it certifies Peace Officers—big difference. Will you help keep the peace by defending the rights of the people you serve or will you not? If not now, when? Ask yourself what it will take for you to make a stand. Are you waiting on an initiative that "goes too far"? Where is your line in the sand? What will it take for YOU to stand up and say, "NO, I can't enforce this because it violates citizens' rights!"? When you remember your oath to defend the people's rights, it's a conflict of interest to enforce a flawed law. In light of this information, I hope that we can move past the statement that because you are "law enforcement" you must enforce the law. Remember Rosa Parks and the millions of Jews who lost their lives because of that thinking. Don't be that cop.

Another troubling comment I have heard from police leaders is: "I'm waiting to see what the state police chiefs and sheriffs' association or the courts say before I make a decision."

My answer to this comment may seem a little harsh to some, but it is critical that this point gets made if for nothing else, maybe a little self-reflection. Only the guilty need feel guilty. If you have made the above statement or agree with it, you need to take a long hard look in the mirror and here's why.

Are you a leader in your community or are you just another member of the pack? If you need to have a group behind you and you feel more confident in numbers then you may not be the sheepdog, but just a sheep in the flock. Here is why I think this way.

You are meant to be a leader, the protector of the citizens you serve, not a follower. The people you serve and protect hired you and they deserve better. They deserve someone with the intestinal fortitude and courage to stand alone for them, if necessary. Be the one leading not a member of the herd. Too often, the crowd is wrong or doesn't have the guts or the will it takes to make a stand and "go against the grain" if necessary. It's easier to "go along to get along" and stand in the shadows (believe me I can relate). Our founding fathers stood up and fought, and many died for our precious liberties and rights! Remember how much they risked forming our great nation.

There should be no question in your mind that I1639 infringes on citizens' rights protected by the 2nd Amendment of the U.S. Constitution and Article 24 of the Washington State Constitution. If you are honest with yourself, you don't need the courts, attorneys, police chiefs or sheriffs to tell you what to do. If you need someone else to think for you in order for you to take a stand, then please reconsider your position as law enforcement. The people you serve need someone with a moral compass who will stand up for them against abuses of their rights, no matter what. The "cost" of making a stand is nothing compared to the sacrifices our founders and military have given defending our rights and way of life since our country's inception.

"It is natural for a man to indulge in the illusions of hope. We are apt to shut our eyes against a painful

truth—and listen to the song of that siren till she transforms us into beasts. Is this the part of wise men, engaged in a great and arduous struggle for liberty? Are we disposed to be of the number of those who, having eyes, see not, and having ears, hear not, the things which so nearly concern their temporal salvation? For my part, whatever anguish of spirit it might cost, I am willing to know the whole truth; to know the worst and to provide for it."
– Patrick Henry

Chapter 8

GOD, FAMILY, COUNTRY, PATRIOTISM

*"A spirit of liberty and patriotism animates
all degrees and denominations of men."*
– James Madison

Like most Americans, my family has always been very patriotic. We love the American Flag, and we love our country. The flag represents the United States and has flown around the world during every war. Active duty military, police, and veterans who have died are seen in flag-draped coffins.

Police work is in my blood. My wife's grandfather, Lloyd Daily, was the sheriff here in Ferry County, Washington for about two decades back in the 60s and 70s. My dad, Rod Culp, was a Washington State Patrol trooper, a deputy U.S. marshal and a deputy sheriff in Jefferson County, Washington when I was young. We lived just outside of Port Townsend, WA on a small farm located on Marrowstone Island and later lived in a small community known as Chimacum when he was a deputy.

We moved to Republic when I was about 15 years old. I got my work ethic from my dad and from watching my mom, Deeta Drovdahl, work her tail off so we could have better things and a better life. She did an excellent job of raising four boys. She went through tough times that would have broken a weaker person, but she never gave up. Her grit and perseverance helped make me who I am today.

I remember as a small child who could barely see over the dash, going on calls in a police car with my dad in the middle of the night. I always wanted to be a police officer when I grew up. However, my dad left law enforcement about the time I entered high school, and he pursued a career in building homes as a general contractor. I followed him into that profession. It wasn't until later in life that I realized my dream of becoming a police officer. I've been a patrol officer, narcotics detective, sergeant and now chief of police. I wish I would have started police work earlier in my life. Helping people, protecting rights and putting criminals away is gratifying work that I hope to continue for many years. Because of my upbringing and military service, I have much respect for our flag and what it stands for and represents. It always flies proudly at my home.

Many years ago while camping with my family, I made it a habit to raise the flag in the morning and to lower it every evening. I felt inspired at that time to write the following poem about patriotism. I thought it was appropriate to include it in this chapter. I hope you enjoy it.

WHAT WOULD YOU DO FOR A FRIEND?
By Loren Culp

Each morning I move you outside to feel the breeze and sun in your face and to get some fresh air. We've always been together, through thick and thin, because,

That's what you do for a friend.

We served our country with honor, fighting side by side. You were so brave, you never faltered, through your bravery, pride and honor you gave all the men courage and conviction to continue the fight, even against overwhelming odds you stood tall and proud, leading us on to victory.

I was there as you led the charge against our country's enemies, right beside you I fought, because,

That's what you would do for a friend.

My grandchildren know of your stories, I've told them every detail, from our humble beginnings together to the present day, they know all we have been through, because,

That's what you do for a friend.

Now we are old and tattered, but our friendship has never faltered, sure we had our spats and disagreements but through it all, we've stuck together, because,

That's what you would do for a friend.

Now my life has ended, my family has gathered 'round, and as I lay cold and still, you have me covered, as always, because,

That's what you would do for a friend.

As they lower me into the ground, you will return home with my family, and throughout the days and years to come, you will give them comfort and support, through you I will live on forever in their hearts and minds, because,

That's what you do for a friend.

OLD GLORY I thank YOU, you've been a true friend of mine.

We Can't Remain Silent

I am disappointed by the lack of support by Washington police leaders since I publicly demonstrated my desire to protect constitutional rights here in Republic. There are some, however, who have come forward to support OUR rights. If only they say they will not actively enforce this law, it's a step in the right direction. There are far too many people remaining silent and hiding behind the excuses I mentioned, even some condemning my actions.

If you are a citizen, your police chiefs, sheriffs, and representatives need to hear from you. Their phone numbers should be on your phone, and their emails need to be at the ready. Start by finding your voice, which will inspire others to use their voices. It takes guts to do the right thing, and help others find their intestinal fortitude. When is the last time you

Loren with grandson Ruger Culp celebrating freedom.

contacted your representatives in government or your local chief of police or sheriff? These people are your employees and work for you. They need to hear from you regularly, to understand what you want and what concerns you have.

Good communication between citizens and law enforcement can manage expectations and prevent misunderstandings. Do your research and be informed. Find out when town hall meetings are scheduled and go to them. Be involved. Ask questions and see where your law enforcement stands. If their beliefs don't align with yours, then support someone else who will fight for your rights. Pay close attention to the actions taken and not just to promises made. Are they standing against the abuses of your rights? Find out.

This battle I am engaging in, about I1639, is one I took on for the people I work for in the City of Republic, WA. It was not intended to be heard all across this nation and the world, but I am glad it was. Hopefully, the attention will help to educate more people to the dangers of restricting our rights. I was merely doing my job here for my town. Now that it has spread and received national attention, I need your help. I am one voice, one small town police chief. The only thing necessary is for the people, who are supposed to be the protectors of their communities, to protect citizens from the abuses of the mob mentality that is so prevalent in not only I1639 but all initiatives and laws that infringe our rights. As our founders knew, direct democracy, which is the initiative process, is a grave danger to our liberties and must be abolished. Please don't believe the lies and propaganda about the United States being a democracy. It is NOT! You know the truth now. Take action. Call your friends, call your government employees, get this book into the hands of as many people as you can. Could you help me spread the word?

I know firsthand that many sheriffs and police chiefs, like American citizens, do not see this information. Now that you know, be involved and attend town hall meetings. Ask questions and make statements.

Communicate your expectations and educate them. Hand them this book! Ask them to read it and then talk about it. Most in law enforcement are afraid of losing their jobs, but by educating them, you will empower them to stand up against the abuse of our rights. Assure them that they have your support because if more of them feel the people's support, then chances are more may stand up for our rights. Sheriffs and police chiefs have the power to direct their agencies and focus their enforcement and don't need to "wait to see what the courts decide." It is up to the discretion of that agency what they will enforce.

The police are under the executive branch of government, and judges are under the judiciary branch. Neither branch runs the other. Ask yourself if you would accept a police chief or sheriff who is waiting to be "told by a judge" before he takes action? Maybe you need a new chief of police or sheriff?

"For true patriots to be silent, is dangerous."
– Samuel Adams

Chapter 9

A FEW WORDS ABOUT GUN-FREE ZONES

"However weak our country may be, I hope we shall never sacrifice our liberties."
— Alexander Hamilton

"The very atmosphere of firearms anywhere and everywhere restrains evil interference — they deserve a place of honor with all that is good."
— George Washington

When the arguments turn to firearms, many people often site school shootings as a reason to limit firearms. If criminals followed the law, then gun-free zones would be significant. However, judging from my experience as a police officer, criminals don't follow the rules. With the increase in school shootings and other shootings in gun-free zones, that shouldn't be too hard to understand for anyone.

If gun-free zones, gun bans, magazine limitations, and restrictions on attachments stopped shootings and made us safer, then the City of Chicago, for example, would be a safe place. According to the Chicago Tribune, there were about 600 murders in Chicago in 2018, and approximately 3,000 people were shot. Chicago is well-known for having some of the strictest gun laws in the country and yet these statistics are still a fact.

Murder is, and always has been, against the law. Shooting people is, and always has been, against the law. Criminals don't abide by signs that say 'don't bring a gun here' or respect other laws to be good citizens. That is why we have a process to convict them when they violate a law. This is done to protect our society from evil and keep people safe.

Restrictive signs and laws only disarm the law-abiding public and give people the illusion of protection and safety. If I'm a law-abiding citizen, I don't want to be arrested and charged with a crime so I choose to follow the law by not bringing my gun to a gun-free zone. This reasoning leaves all of the good people unarmed and defenseless when a mass shooting happens. Criminals will do what criminals do! They will break the law because they don't care, they are CRIMINALS!

Whoever thought of making gun-free zones in the first place? It is just another "feel-good" law that does nothing to curb crime. It makes everyone a victim by disarming those who would defend others. Need proof? Answer this question: where are most mass shootings taking place? You don't even need time to think about that, do you? No matter your political affiliation, if we are honest with each other we all know that the majority of mass shootings take place in gun-free zones. Mass shooters are cowards and go where the killing is easy. Have you ever seen a mass shooter at a gun show? I wonder why? Mass shooters are cowards, but they aren't stupid.

A more appropriate sign would be: "Multiple people in this facility are armed with a gun and will not hesitate to shoot you dead if you are a threat." Like George Washington said in the above quote, "guns restrain evil everywhere." We need evil restrained; we don't need to make easy "killing fields" with gun-free zones, and we don't need law-abiding citizens or guns restrained because guns aren't the problem! Criminals are the problem, so we should make it harder for criminals to commit crimes, not easier.

Recently, President Trump has been speaking against gun-free zones for the same reasons I've listed. I support him in this and hope he is successful in getting rid of them! It is nonsense that people think a sign will stop anyone but the law-abiding. Good people with guns stop bad people intent on doing harm, plain and simple.

When I was in the U.S. Military, I had the privilege to serve under President Ronald Reagan. President Reagan was a strong supporter of the right to keep and bear arms, even after he had been shot on March 30, 1981, as he was leaving a speaking engagement at a hotel in Washington D.C., a city with some of the most restrictive gun laws in the nation! Years later in 1983, he gave a speech to the National Rifle Association. In that speech, he said the following:

"Those who seek to inflict harm are not fazed by gun control laws. I happen to know this from personal experience."

President Reagan knew the truth, and so do most Americans, especially in the police field, whether they want to admit it or not. If laws kept criminals from committing crimes, then we would be out of a job! It should be glaringly obvious: gun laws do nothing to stop criminals. The only people that follow gun control laws are the law-abiding citizens.

When I was young, we brought guns to school in our vehicles. However, none of us committed a school shooting. We brought them to school because we went hunting before or after classes. We were taught from a young age to respect guns, and our parents taught us how to handle a firearm safely.

Guns haven't changed much, but our culture has. It would take another whole book to talk about the real problem: our culture and our mental health services. Having worked in public service, I can tell you that mental health services in our country need a major overhaul! Almost all of the people responsible for mass shootings were on some form of prescription medication for one mental disorder or another.

Police deal with people who have mental health problems all the time. Unfortunately, without a safe place to take them that will protect them and the public, they are left to roam the streets. Eventually, they may commit a serious crime at the mercy of their mental disorder. As I said, this subject would take up a book of its own, so I'll leave it at that for now.

Chapter 10

A TOWN WITH A CONSTITUTIONAL NAME: THE CITY OF REPUBLIC

"Americans (have) the right and advantage of being armed, unlike citizens of other countries whose governments are afraid to trust the people with arms." – James Madison

"Arms discourage and keep the invader and plunderer in awe, and preserve order in the world as well as property...Horrid mischief would ensue were the law-abiding deprived of the use of them." – Thomas Paine

I told you earlier in this book I would brag on my town a little bit. So here we go! Republic, Washington, the city with the name of our form of government, still has an early 1900s look and feel to it. It is where I currently serve as the Police Chief and where I lived during most of my high school years. It is where I met my wife back in 1976 before we got married and left for our adventure called life.

Loren with future wife Barb in Republic yearbook.

Like most small-town kids, we couldn't wait to leave Republic and see what the world had to offer. It didn't take long to realize we needed to get back to the mountains and the peaceful, quiet life of home.

We soon missed the small town and spent years trying to get back here. Republic hasn't changed much since then. Many of the buildings here are from the very

Mountains surround Republic, WA.

early years. Republic was founded by gold prospectors; its original name was Eureka Gulch. In the late 1800s, gold was found in the area, and a boomtown began.

Republic is the county seat of Ferry County and boasts a population of just over 1,000 people. I remember a show on TV many years ago called "Cheers"; the theme song said, "where everybody knows your name." Well, that would definitely be Republic.

It is a "hub of activity" with a pharmacy, hardware store, hospital, several churches, a brewery, hotels, grocery store, courthouse, and local restaurants. There is an active shooting range within a quarter mile of the city limits where citizens go to practice shooting or sighting in their guns. It gets much use just before hunting season. The gun range is also used by the U.S. Border Patrol and local police for practice and weapons qualifications.

Republic is right between two mountain passes, Wauconda to the west and Sherman to the east. Sherman pass is the highest year-around pass in Washington State with an elevation of about 5,574 feet. Both are very scenic, and Sherman pass has several parking areas where travelers can take in the view. Both passes are drivable year around on State Highway 20, which goes right through the center of town.

There is much to do in and around Republic. There is a fossil site where you can dig and discover ancient fossils with just a little effort at the Stone Rose Fossil Site just a block from downtown. We may not be a metropolis, but you won't be bored!

Fishing or water skiing are big on Curlew Lake. The views in the Republic area are second to none. Mountains, trees, rivers, and lakes are all over the place and a sight to behold. There are also many smaller lakes in the area higher up in the mountains such as Empire, Swan, Ferry, and Fish lakes, all reachable by car with campgrounds at most places. There are several resorts or lodges around Republic including the Konz Ranch just south of town close to the San Poil River. Curlew Lake has resorts with rental cabins, boats, and docks. The lakes in the area are well-stocked with fish.

A TOWN WITH A CONSTITUTIONAL NAME: THE CITY OF REPUBLIC

There is an abundance of wildlife also: mule deer, whitetail deer, moose, elk, black bears, cougars, bobcats, beavers, muskrats, ermines, badgers, coyotes, bighorn sheep, and wolves. The deer population draws hunting families from everywhere during hunting season.

There is also a "rail trail." Years ago the railroad pulled out of Republic after the lumber mill closed. Now it is a hiking/biking trail, used by many, with parts of it going from Republic and around the west side of Curlew Lake to the railroad trestle. Just north of Republic is the small community of Curlew which is right next to the Kettle River. There is lots of history there, and they have their own museum.

There is a state park on the east side of Curlew Lake that is maintained very nicely with large grassy areas to picnic and play, a swimming area and a dock with a boat ramp. If you ever go to Curlew Lake, be sure to say hi to Ranger Rick Sanders. He is responsible for the beautiful park.

Despite its 2,200 square mile area, Ferry County has a tiny tax base since nearly half of the county is part of the Colville Indian Reservation. Much of the rest of the county is part of the Colville National Forest. This leaves less than 20% of the county in taxable land. Tons of recreational opportunities everywhere but there is very little income for policing and other government responsibilities. A stroll around downtown Republic will take you back in time as you check out the many old buildings and shops along Clark Avenue, our "main" street named after one of the founders of Republic.

If you find yourself visiting Republic on vacation, be sure to stop in and say hi. Just ask anyone you see, and they will tell you either where I'm at or how to get in touch with me.

Chapter 11

MY HOPE

"The two enemies of the people are criminals and government, so let us tie the second down with the chains of the Constitution so the second will not become the legalized version of the first."
– Thomas Jefferson

My ultimate goal in writing this book was to make you more informed and perhaps inspired to think. I hope that with that inspiration and the little knowledge that you may have gained it will help you to take a stand with thousands of patriotic Americans and me all across this great country.

We as a nation are looking for leaders, someone who is willing to step up and stand for what is right no matter what!

If you are in the police profession, then that is you. If you are a police leader then you direct where your police force will focus its work on a daily basis, so it is most certainly you. If you are not in a leadership position, but are a police officer, then get this book in the hands of your supervisors and other officers. Open up the discussion with them, respectfully.

You have an obligation, reinforced by your oath of office, to not violate citizens' constitutional rights. Don't be that officer who would arrest Rosa Parks "because it's the law"!

If you are a citizen who wants to see your police or sheriff make a stand and defend your rights, then contact them. Contact your county commissioners and city council members, give them this book, have a conversation. Our country needs you NOW! This is the action that is required by we the people. Our rights are under attack, and it is not going to let up until the legislative bodies, police, and sheriffs nullify infringements on constitutional rights by saying NO, we will not violate someone's rights no matter what.

I could have written a lengthy book, added more pages of "fluff," expounded on the ideas, ad nauseam, but keep this in mind: the Declaration of Independence was only 4,558 words. And yet, it is one of the most historic and beautiful yet pointed documents ever written. It gets right to the point; it delivered the message in a clear and concise way without the "fluff." I'm not one to enjoy lengthy powerpoint presentations or long drawn-out meetings with people who like to hear their voices (believe me there are plenty of those in public service).

I like to get to the subject at hand. If there is a problem, I will fix it. I spent 20 years running my own construction business where "time is money." I've found that too many people in public service feel the need to talk more and do less. So I guess my thinking comes from making the best of my time and yours. Adding pages just for the sake of adding pages is a waste of your time, my time and paper.

Public servants need to remember that their time is YOUR money. I hope that this book has delivered to you a clear message and I hope it spurs you into action because your country needs you! Feel free to contact me with your comments, good or bad. "Let's do what we do."

Email: bluelineloren@gmail.com

WE MUST REMAIN ETERNALLY VIGILANT! May God Bless you and keep you safe and may God Bless America! Your friend in "Eternal Vigilance"

– Loren Culp

"The price of freedom is eternal vigilance."
– Thomas Jefferson

Chapter 12

BONUS UPDATE FROM LOREN CULP

I wrote the majority of this book in December of 2018 and it was available on Amazon in just over one month from the time I finished it. It became a #1 best seller on Amazon.com in three categories. It was #1 on the hot 100 new books list for weeks. It is now September of 2019. A lot has happened since I took a stand for you, the citizen, and got this vital information out to the public. I spent the first six months of this year traveling around Washington State on my days off to various events I was invited to. I've spoken to many groups about our rights and about our heritage as Americans. I've signed a lot of books and made a lot of new friends along the way. It has been an amazing journey throughout. One thing that started happening while I was doing my book tour is, people started asking me to run for governor of Washington State. I have never been a candidate for office but as I continued to speak across this State, more and more people urged me to run.

They told me that they are sick of politicians and want someone in office who will keep their word by upholding and defending the Constitution and citizens' rights. About a month ago, I gave a speech at the Republic City Park. I was introduced by Klickitat County Sheriff Bob Songer. Sheriff Songer is also a firm believer in our founding documents and drove six hours, one way, to be at this event and show his support. I said the following, in that speech:

"Thank you all for being here; this is incredible. If someone would have told me as a young man growing up here in Republic Washington that this would be happening right now, I would have told them they were crazy.

But my name is Loren Culp and I am running to be the governor of Washington State!

I have never run for political office, so, you might ask, why am I doing it now? Well, I'll tell you why. I'm sick and tired, as I know many of you are, of seeing career politician after career politician trampling on our rights and spending our money like a drunken sailor. And I mean no disrespect to any drunken sailors who might be with us today; we love our veterans.

As many of you know, I stood up against the unconstitutional anti-gun initiative 1639 in November of 2018. If there is anyone left on this planet, besides Attorney General Bob Ferguson and Washington Governor Jay Inslee, who doesn't believe it's unconstitutional to restrict someone's God-given rights, then look up Section 24 of the Washington State Constitution and have a 6th grader tell you what it means, because it's one simple sentence. 'The right of the individual citizen to bear arms in defense of himself or the State shall not be impaired.' If anyone believes that the constitution doesn't protect the right to own a semiautomatic rifle because they weren't invented when it was written, then I guess the same thing applies to typewriters, computers and the internet when it comes to the 1st Amendment.

If you think that any law that restricts the rights of law abiding citizens is going to have any influence on a criminal that's intent on doing someone harm, then why hasn't the law against committing murder taken care of the problem? Criminals don't obey the law. Rest assured folks, it's not about making us safer, it's about control. All you have to do is look at history. Jay Inslee and Bob Ferguson intentionally misled the voters of this state and they continue to push laws restricting citizen's rights to this day and they are proud of it! I have personally talked to some of those voters that were misled and they aren't happy. In fact they are downright mad about being misled.

Martin Luther King said and I quote:

> *There are two types of laws: just and unjust. I would be the first to advocate obeying just laws. One has not only a legal but a moral responsibility to obey just laws. Conversely, one has a moral responsibility to disobey unjust laws.*

Rosa parks would never have been arrested and taken to jail if the police would have understood this principle, and millions of Jews would have not been marched to their deaths in Germany.

I was thrust into the national spotlight because of my position on this. I became a voice for you, not by my planning and not by my design. It just happened. You see, I took a public oath—not once, not twice, but three times. Once in the US army, once as a police officer and once as the Chief of Police. That promise that I made when I took that oath was to you, my friends and my family. I promised that I would uphold and defend the constitution of the United States and the Constitution of the State of Washington. I have kept that promise, even at the risk of my career, because I believe in keeping my word and I believe in our founding documents.

Before anyone takes office they say the same oath. Sadly, far too many don't keep their word to you. They go through the motions and repeat the words, but five minutes later they forget all about it. That oath is not to one amendment or one part of the Constitution; it's to the whole thing. The beauty of our founding documents is that they protect everyone equally, but only if they are followed by elected officials and the police.

The Declaration of Independence says that governments are instituted to protect citizens' rights. That is the role of government. It's not the role of government to take care of us from the cradle to the grave. If you elect me as your next governor I will ensure that any bill crossing my desk will pass three tests. Is it Constitutional? Is it needed? And do we have the money to pay for it?

I don't care if you are a Democrat or a Republican, liberal or conservative or somewhere in-between. We are all citizens of Washington State. Most of us have the same goals in life. Live peacefully, love our friends and family, work hard and if we are lucky, live long enough to retire. But in the process of that we don't need a bloated government in Olympia telling us what to do at every turn and taxing us like there is no limit.

If you elect me as your next governor I will be a governor for all of the people of Washington State. I will work tirelessly to reduce the size and scope of government interference in our lives and businesses. I will work tirelessly to make your government much more efficient. What we currently have is a disgrace. When I took over as the Chief of Police right here in Republic we cut about twenty-five percent from the police department budget in the first month, saving the tax payers about $120,000 per year. That is a huge amount for a small town and it can be done at the State level as well!

Free people don't need government telling them what to do all the time. If you elect me, you will have a governor who respects the rule of law and respects citizens' rights as outlined in our Constitution. That is my promise to you and I have a pretty good track record of keeping my word!

I'm just a common man, willing to work for common people, for a common purpose, which is freedom! Freedom from high taxes. Freedom from excessive regulations. Freedom from a government in Olympia that doesn't share the same values that we do.

Now, I have no experience being a politician. I have no doubt that my opponents, whoever they may be, will try to use that against me. But career politicians have been running things for decades in this State, and look where we are. What have you got to lose by giving me a chance to fix things using common sense with a business background? Restrictive laws, high taxes, massive regulations, human feces on the sidewalks of our major cities, dirty needles laying around and criminals that go through a revolving door or don't get charged to begin with.

We currently have a governor who is running around the United States acting like we don't notice he is spending millions of our tax dollars for his vanity run for President. By the way, I think Governor Jay Inslee and I are tied in the race for President and I'm not even running.

Jay Inslee says it's lawful for him to spend millions in tax payer money for his campaign. But remember Martin Luther King's quote? Is it a just law, Mr. Inslee? Is it just for you to spend the people's money like you are for your own ambitions? I can't imagine, even if it was lawful, for me to ask the citizens of Republic to pay my salary for a job, if I wasn't here doing it, but not only that, pay extra for my security detail like he is.

Have you had enough of career politicians yet?! I sure have and I think you have too. Our founders didn't have experience running a free country but they had the will, the determination and the common sense to get it done and they did a damn fine job!

I will probably make some mistakes along the way. I don't have degrees from an Ivy league university to hang on my wall. I don't have millions of dollars in the bank. But what I do have is common sense and a strong work ethic. Common sense isn't something you can learn from reading a book or taking a class. It is so lacking in our state's leadership right now. Common sense is what I have and what I will bring to the table as your next governor.

Folks, we are citizens of America, right, left, conservative, liberal, black, white, and brown; it doesn't matter to me. We are all one state, we are all part of one nation and we are all one people. I plan on representing all residents of Washington State. We have become so divisive lately. Some have forgotten what it means to be an American and how to have a dialogue with each other about issues we may differ on. We can still be different and have different points of view on things but we can still respect each other.

Let me tell you a true story. When I was a Sergeant in the U.S. Army in 1983, I was stationed in South

Korea for 357 days straight. My little boys didn't even recognize who I was when I got home. While I was there I participated in a joint military exercise called Team Spirit. All of the branches of the US military along with South Korean Forces were involved. It was huge. There were ships and tanks and aircraft all around the country. We would travel long distances in large army trucks and jeeps along small dirt roads, all around Korea. There were small villages dotted along the roads in the countryside and all of them were surrounded by rice paddies.

When the convoys of trucks loaded with GIs and equipment would get close to a village, all of the people who lived there, including little children, would hear the trucks coming and they would all run up and line the edge of the road. They would wave to us with one hand, big smiles on their faces and in their other hand they waved small American flags as we drove by. They didn't care what race or political affiliation the men and women were inside the trucks. They cared about what we represented. What we meant to them. What we stood for, which was freedom and liberty. We need to remember here at home to stand up for that same freedom and liberty, something that people in other countries realize more so than we do sometimes.

We need to get back to the basics, folks. Back to what made this country so great which is a small, nonintrusive, simple government. A government that isn't involved in your daily lives with its hand in your pocket.

Back to what our founders said in the Declaration of Independence, that government was created to protect citizen's rights.

If you elect me as your governor, I promise you I will fight for smaller government every single day! Somebody once said 'A government that can give you everything you want can take everything you have.' And it's true—you can't have freedom and liberty with a big bloated government ruling over you!

I've been married to my wife Barb for forty-one years this year. I was a small business owner for over twenty years starting in 1988 in the Olympia area. I know the struggles of running a business. I started out with a 1976 Datsun pickup that I bought from my Grandpa for $600. I started my business doing concrete foundations around Olympia. I had to make multiple trips in that old small truck to get the concrete forms moved from one job site to another and I only had one employee at the time. But I was free, working for myself, experiencing the American dream. I built that business up from nothing to having multiple trucks and multiple employees doing big and small projects all around Puget Sound. My youngest son, Adam, still runs that business to this day.

Government didn't help me do that; government hindered me with taxes and regulations and it's gotten a lot worse since then. Ask any small business owner in this state and they will tell you that taxes and regulations make it very hard on them and many struggle to keep the doors open. I'm not anti-government but I am anti-big government.

When was the last time you heard of taxes being lowered and rules and regulations being cut in this state? Never—taxes keep getting higher and regulations more restrictive. Our state government acts like we work for them instead of the other way around. That will change when I'm elected! Less taxes and less regulations lead to more individual freedom and that's something all Washingtonians should embrace.

Let's talk about the so called 'Homeless Crisis' for a minute.

I could say so much about this. First of all, I don't agree with the term Homeless Crisis. I don't believe there is a problem with homes. I believe there is a problem with mental health and addiction. Here is where common sense comes into play. If you reward bad behavior, you get more of it. That's what is going on right now under the nose of Jay Inslee and Bob Ferguson. Seattle and other places around Puget Sound have stopped arresting and charging anyone with three grams or less of heroin. That is a felony in this state and they are ignoring it.

What would attract more heroin users to an area more than not having any punishment for possessing and using heroin? Nothing! And guess what? The drug dealers who are pushing this poison adjust to this new policy and only carry small amounts on them at a time. That is what is going on with this so called "homeless crisis." Reward bad behavior and you get more of it.

Not only that but we as tax payers supplement their income with EBT cards and welfare. Why don't we have random drug testing for people on public assistance like we do for people who work for a living? Isn't that common sense?

Tough enforcement and compassionate treatment is what is necessary for people with addictions to get clean. That is what has worked here in Republic and that's what can work on a bigger scale all across the state. There is no bigger reward than to have experienced what I have here as a police officer. Many people hate me when they get arrested and taken to jail for narcotics crimes.

They are forced into treatment by the courts. When they finish treatment, get clean and get their family back, and their life back, they tell me I saved their lives and they are very thankful. I've experienced that multiple times in my police career here in Republic. That's how you show compassion, with tough love.

On the other hand our state's attorney general turns a blind eye to these felonies because he prefers to go after constitutionally protected rights and sue President Trump. Meanwhile these people continue to suffer in addiction and they are joined by more and more people from different places around the country because they won't face consequences in Seattle. That is why the streets are filling up with tents, feces and needles.

Mental health facilities in this state are a joke. For example, Western State hospital has a budget to upgrade the infrastructure of the hospital that treats the mentally ill to the tune of over thirty million dollars. Twenty-three million has already been spent, and nothing works. Who is in charge of this? Jay Inslee! Who is being held accountable for this waste? Have you heard? No one that I know of. This is gross mismanagement.

When the police pick someone up who has tried to kill themselves, most of the time there is no place for them to go, so they are sent home after only a couple hours. Does that sound like common sense to you? These people are crying out for help but sorry, the state is wasting millions and has no place for you to get help. This can't continue; it is absolutely unacceptable.

I could go on and on but I won't because you've got better things to do with your day. I'm not the type of person who likes to hear myself talk. I prefer action over words. Lots of politicians can talk circles around people until you forget what they are even talking about. I think they prefer that but I'm not that way; I will tell you directly how I feel or I'll think on it and get back to you. That may upset some people but that's the way I am. I don't want to talk things to death. I want to get to work and I will work for you like no one you have ever seen, if you give me the chance. I know the answers to these problems; it's just good old-fashioned common sense, folks.

It's going to take a lot to turn this ship around but we are about to hit the rocks if we don't. We need donations to make this happen; there are no two ways about that.

Even small donations will add up. You can go to our website at Culpforgovernor.com and donate online.

I do have some good news though. The citizens of Washington State are not alone in this, folks. We are getting individual donations from all across the United States. People in Alaska have joined our fight. California and Oregon have joined our fight. Vermont and Florida have sent financial help. America is watching what we are doing right now, and ladies and gentlemen, we are going to make history right here from the tiny town of Republic Washington!

People in other states are helping because they care about freedom and liberty just as much as we do even though this isn't their state. Freedom resonates with all Americans. And guess what part of Washington has the most people donating right now? From Everett to Tacoma and the greater Seattle area—that is where the most donations are coming from right now. That is amazing and I haven't even talked to any major news outlets in Eastern Washington yet. This is going to be huge and I'm so glad you are all a part of it.

May God Bless America and May God Bless Washington State! So, who's ready to send common sense to Olympia!? Let's do what we do!"

When I was done, the crowd erupted into cheers and applause. We are about a month into this campaign for governor and things are going very well. Time will tell where this journey ends, but once again I find myself standing up for what's right and I will never back down. We have a website up; Culpforgovernor.com. No matter where you are in the United States, if you are a citizen who loves freedom and everything our great country stands for like I do, I need your help. I am *asking* for your help. Please help me take this once great state back from the far left who have it in their firm grasp. America needs you; I need you. Please go to Culpforgovernor.com now and make a contribution to help me fight and win. I thank you for helping me stand up for our founding principles. With your help we WILL take this country back, one state at a time. God Bless you and God Bless America!

ABOUT THE AUTHOR

I am the current police chief of a small picturesque mountain town in northeastern Washington State called "The City of Republic." It is a beautiful place, and I'm proud to call it home. There are only eight paid employees of the City, including Mayor Elbert Koontz; three at City Hall, three at public works and two in the Police Department.

I've been married to my high school sweetheart, Barbara (Clough), for over forty years. We first met in high school here in Republic. I played football in high school until my second injury put me out of the game for good. Barb and I had two boys together, now grown men with their own families; Nicholas and Adam. They have blessed us with seven grandchildren ranging in age from one to seventeen.

I have been on my own since I was seventeen years old, living in a one bedroom apartment that was once part of the old hospital in downtown Republic. The City of Republic hasn't changed much since then, and that's one reason we still love it here.

I worked in construction before joining the U.S. Army in the summer of 1980. After attending Drill Sergeant School as a Corporal at Fort Leonard Wood Missouri, I helped train new army recruits, turning civilians into soldiers. It was rewarding to know that I played a part in turning these people into soldiers. I will cherish the memories I have of my time serving this great country. When I wasn't training recruits, my job in the military was as a combat engineer (explosives and heavy equipment operator). Eventually, I achieved the rank of Sergeant.

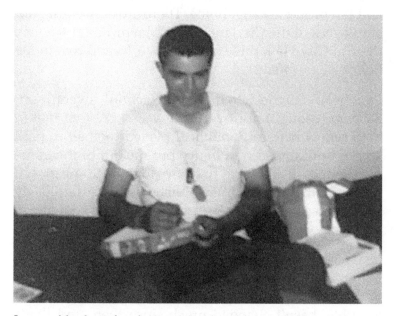

Loren writing home from basic training the old fashioned way in 1980.

I served under President Ronald Reagan in the 101st Airborne Division at Fort Campbell Kentucky, 2nd Infantry Division in Korea and the 6th Air Cavalry at Fort Hood Texas. I qualified as an expert with hand grenades and the M16 rifle.

I was the honor graduate of my military occupational specialty (MOS) class, and later I was an honor graduate of the NCO (Non-Commissioned Officer) Academy.

After serving four years in the Army, I went back to construction and in 1989 started my own General Contracting business in the Olympia Washington area where I built homes, rental properties and did concrete work for 20 years. Olympia is also where I learned to fly airplanes and received my private pilot's license.

After moving back to this area some years ago, I saw an ad in the local newspaper advertising for a police officer position in the City of Republic. My childhood dreams could now be a reality; I answered that ad and put in my application. At the age of forty-nine, I met the physical and mental challenges in the police academy while training with a class made up of mostly young men and women twenty years my junior.

Since then I have served the Republic community as a patrol officer, narcotics detective, sergeant and I am currently a Narcotics and Patrol K9 Handler, as well as the Chief of Police. I'm now working with my second K9 Karma (pictured on the back cover) after my beloved K9 Isko died unexpectedly last year. I have worked with some fantastic officers over the years, too many to list, but I am eternally grateful for their help, commitment and work ethic.

Since this book launched on President's Day in February 2019, I have traveled the state sharing my message in support of our Constitutional Rights. As fate would have it, many providential doors have opened. I had no idea then that I would be running a full-scale gubernatorial campaign less than a year later. This responsibility is something I take very seriously and I hope that by taking an active role in politics, we can restore faith in our country and defend the founding documents that guarantee our freedoms and the pursuit of our happiness. Thank you for your continued support. Please share this book with someone you love and please get out and vote.

My life has been quite an adventure so far, but one thing is for sure: it is never too late to follow your dreams!

> *"Is life so dear, or peace so sweet, as to be purchased at the price of chains and slavery?*
>
> *Forbid it, Almighty God! I know not what course others may take; but as for me, give me liberty or give me death!" – Patrick Henry*

APPENDIX

DECLARATION OF INDEPENDENCE

[Adopted in Congress 4 July 1776]

The Unanimous Declaration of the Thirteen United States of America

When, in the course of human events, it becomes necessary for one people to dissolve the political bands which have connected them with another, and to assume among the powers of the earth, the separate and equal station to which the laws of nature and of nature's God entitle them, a decent respect to the opinions of mankind requires that they should declare the causes which impel them to the separation.

We hold these truths to be self-evident, that all men are created equal, that they are endowed by their Creator with certain unalienable rights, that among these are life, liberty and the pursuit of happiness. That to secure these rights, governments are instituted among men, deriving their just powers from the consent of the governed. That whenever any form of government becomes destructive of these ends, it is the right of the people to alter or to abolish it, and to institute new government, laying its foundation on such principles and organizing its powers in such form, as to them shall seem most likely to effect their safety and happiness. Prudence, indeed, will dictate that governments long established should not be changed for light and transient causes; and accordingly all experience hath shown that mankind are more disposed to suffer, while evils are sufferable, than to right themselves by abolishing the forms to which they are accustomed. But when a long train of abuses and usurpations, pursuing invariably the same object evinces a design to reduce them under absolute despotism, it is their right, it is their duty, to throw off such government, and to provide new guards for their future security. -- Such has been the patient sufferance of these colonies; and such is now the necessity which constrains them to alter their former systems of government. The history of the present King of Great Britain is a history of repeated injuries and usurpations, all having in direct object the establishment of an absolute tyranny over these states. To prove this, let facts be submitted to a candid world.

He has refused his assent to laws, the most wholesome and necessary for the public good.

He has forbidden his governors to pass laws of immediate and pressing importance, unless suspended in their operation till his assent should be obtained; and when so suspended, he has utterly neglected to attend to them.

He has refused to pass other laws for the accommodation of large districts of people, unless those people would relinquish the right of representation in the legislature, a right inestimable to them and formidable to tyrants only.

He has called together legislative bodies at places unusual, uncomfortable, and distant from the depository of their public records, for the sole purpose of fatiguing them into compliance with his measures.

He has dissolved representative houses repeatedly, for opposing with manly firmness his invasions on the rights of the people.

He has refused for a long time, after such dissolutions, to cause others to be elected; whereby the legislative powers, incapable of annihilation, have returned to the people at large for their exercise; the state remaining in the meantime exposed to all the dangers of invasion from without, and convulsions within.

He has endeavored to prevent the population of these states; for that purpose obstructing the laws for naturalization of foreigners; refusing to pass others to encourage their migration hither, and raising the conditions of new appropriations of lands.

He has obstructed the administration of justice, by refusing his assent to laws for establishing judiciary powers.

He has made judges dependent on his will alone, for the tenure of their offices, and the amount and payment of their salaries.

He has erected a multitude of new offices, and sent hither swarms of officers to harass our people, and eat out their substance.

He has kept among us, in times of peace, standing armies without the consent of our legislature.

He has affected to render the military independent of and superior to civil power.

He has combined with others to subject us to a jurisdiction foreign to our constitution, and unacknowledged by our laws; giving his assent to their acts of pretended legislation:

For quartering large bodies of armed troops among us:

For protecting them, by mock trial, from punishment for any murders which they should commit on the inhabitants of these states:

For cutting off our trade with all parts of the world:

For imposing taxes on us without our consent:

For depriving us in many cases, of the benefits of trial by jury:

For transporting us beyond seas to be tried for pretended offenses:

For abolishing the free system of English laws in a neighboring province, establishing therein an arbitrary government, and enlarging its boundaries so as to render it at once an example and fit instrument for introducing the same absolute rule in these colonies:

For taking away our charters, abolishing our most valuable laws, and altering fundamentally the forms of our governments:

For suspending our own legislatures, and declaring themselves invested with power to legislate for us in all cases whatsoever.

He has abdicated government here, by declaring us out of his protection and waging war against us.

He has plundered our seas, ravaged our coasts, burned our towns, and destroyed the lives of our people.

He is at this time transporting large armies of foreign mercenaries to complete the works of death, desolation and tyranny, already begun with circumstances of cruelty and perfidy scarcely paralleled in the most barbarous ages, and totally unworthy of the head of a civilized nation.

He has constrained our fellow citizens taken captive on the high seas to bear arms against their country, to become the executioners of their friends and brethren, or to fall themselves by their hands.

He has excited domestic insurrections amongst us, and has endeavored to bring on the inhabitants of our frontiers, the merciless Indian savages, whose known rule of warfare, is undistinguished destruction of all ages, sexes and conditions.

In every stage of these oppressions we have petitioned for redress in the most humble terms: our repeated petitions have been answered only by repeated injury. A prince, whose character is thus marked by every act which may define a tyrant, is unfit to be the ruler of a free people.

Nor have we been wanting in attention to our British brethren. We have warned them from time to time of attempts by their legislature to extend an unwarrantable jurisdiction over us. We have reminded them of the circumstances of our emigration and settlement here. We have appealed to their native justice and magnanimity, and we have conjured them by the ties of our common kindred to disavow these usurpations, which, would inevitably interrupt our connections and correspondence. They too have been deaf to the voice of justice and of consanguinity. We must, therefore, acquiesce in the necessity, which denounces our separation, and hold them, as we hold the rest of mankind, enemies in war, in peace friends.

We, therefore, the representatives of the United States of America, in General Congress, assembled, appealing to the Supreme Judge of the world for the rectitude of our intentions, do, in the name, and by the authority of the good people of these colonies, solemnly publish and declare, that these united colonies are, and of right ought to be free and independent states; that they are absolved from all allegiance to the British Crown, and that all political connection between them and the state of Great Britain, is and ought to be totally dissolved; and that as free and independent states, they have full power to levey war, conclude peace, contract alliances, establish commerce, and to do all other acts and things which independent states may of right do. And for the support of this declaration, with a firm reliance on the protection of Divine Providence, we mutually pledge to each other our lives, our fortunes and our sacred honor.

U.S. CONSTITUTION

We the People of the United States, in Order to form a more perfect Union, establish Justice, insure domestic Tranquility, provide for the common defence, promote the general Welfare, and secure the Blessings of Liberty to ourselves and our Posterity, do ordain and establish this Constitution for the United States of America.

Article 1.

Section 1

All legislative Powers herein granted shall be vested in a Congress of the United States, which shall consist of a Senate and House of Representatives.

Section 2

The House of Representatives shall be composed of Members chosen every second Year by the People of the several States, and the Electors in each State shall have the Qualifications requisite for Electors of the most numerous Branch of the State Legislature.

No Person shall be a Representative who shall not have attained to the Age of twenty five Years, and been seven Years a Citizen of the United States, and who shall not, when elected, be an Inhabitant of that State in which he shall be chosen.

Representatives and direct Taxes shall be apportioned among the several States which may be included within this Union, according to their respective Numbers, which shall be determined by adding to the whole Number of free Persons, including those bound to Service for a Term of Years, and excluding Indians not taxed, three fifths of all other Persons.

The actual Enumeration shall be made within three Years after the first Meeting of the Congress of the United States, and within every subsequent Term of ten Years, in such Manner as they shall by Law direct. The Number of Representatives shall not exceed one for every thirty Thousand, but each State shall have at Least one Representative; and until such enumeration shall be made, the State of New Hampshire shall be entitled to choose three, Massachusetts eight, Rhode Island and Providence Plantations one, Connecticut five, New York six, New Jersey four, Pennsylvania eight, Delaware one, Maryland six, Virginia ten, North Carolina five, South Carolina five and Georgia three.

When vacancies happen in the Representation from any State, the Executive Authority thereof shall issue Writs of Election to fill such Vacancies.

The House of Representatives shall choose their Speaker and other Officers; and shall have the sole Power of Impeachment.

Section 3

The Senate of the United States shall be composed of two Senators from each State, chosen by the Legislature thereof, for six Years; and each Senator shall have one Vote.

Immediately after they shall be assembled in Consequence of the first Election, they shall be divided as equally as may be into three Classes. The Seats of the Senators of the first Class shall be vacated at the Expiration of the second Year, of the second Class at the Expiration of the fourth Year, and of the third Class at the Expiration of the sixth Year, so that one third may be chosen every second Year; and if Vacancies happen by Resignation, or otherwise, during the Recess of the Legislature of any State, the Executive thereof may make temporary Appointments until the next Meeting of the Legislature, which shall then fill such Vacancies.

No person shall be a Senator who shall not have attained to the Age of thirty Years, and been nine Years a Citizen of the United States, and who shall not, when elected, be an Inhabitant of that State for which he shall be chosen.

The Vice President of the United States shall be President of the Senate, but shall have no Vote, unless they be equally divided.

The Senate shall choose their other Officers, and also a President pro tempore, in the absence of the Vice

President, or when he shall exercise the Office of President of the United States.

The Senate shall have the sole Power to try all Impeachments. When sitting for that Purpose, they shall be on Oath or Affirmation. When the President of the United States is tried, the Chief Justice shall preside: And no Person shall be convicted without the Concurrence of two thirds of the Members present.

Judgment in Cases of Impeachment shall not extend further than to removal from Office, and disqualification to hold and enjoy any Office of honor, Trust or Profit under the United States: but the Party convicted shall nevertheless be liable and subject to Indictment, Trial, Judgment and Punishment, according to Law.

Section 4

The Times, Places and Manner of holding Elections for Senators and Representatives, shall be prescribed in each State by the Legislature thereof; but the Congress may at any time by Law make or alter such Regulations, except as to the Place of Choosing Senators.

The Congress shall assemble at least once in every Year, and such Meeting shall be on the first Monday in December, unless they shall by Law appoint a different Day.

Section 5

Each House shall be the Judge of the Elections, Returns and Qualifications of its own Members, and a Majority of each shall constitute a Quorum to do Business; but a smaller number may adjourn from day to day, and may be authorized to compel the Attendance of absent Members, in such Manner, and under such Penalties as each House may provide.

Each House may determine the Rules of its Proceedings, punish its Members for disorderly Behavior, and, with the Concurrence of two-thirds, expel a Member.

Each House shall keep a Journal of its Proceedings, and from time to time publish the same, excepting such Parts as may in their Judgment require Secrecy; and the Yeas and Nays of the Members of either House on any question shall, at the Desire of one fifth of those Present, be entered on the Journal.

Neither House, during the Session of Congress, shall, without the Consent of the other, adjourn for more than three days, nor to any other Place than that in which the two Houses shall be sitting.

Section 6

The Senators and Representatives shall receive a Compensation for their Services, to be ascertained by Law, and paid out of the Treasury of the United States. They shall in all Cases, except Treason, Felony and

Breach of the Peace, be privileged from Arrest during their Attendance at the Session of their respective Houses, and in going to and returning from the same; and for any Speech or Debate in either House, they shall not be questioned in any other Place.

No Senator or Representative shall, during the Time for which he was elected, be appointed to any civil Office under the Authority of the United States which shall have been created, or the Emoluments whereof shall have been increased during such time; and no Person holding any Office under the United States, shall be a Member of either House during his Continuance in Office.

Section 7

All bills for raising Revenue shall originate in the House of Representatives; but the Senate may propose or concur with Amendments as on other Bills.

Every Bill which shall have passed the House of Representatives and the Senate, shall, before it become a Law, be presented to the President of the United States; If he approve he shall sign it, but if not he shall return it, with his Objections to that House in which it shall have originated, who shall enter the Objections at large on their Journal, and proceed to reconsider it. If after such Reconsideration two thirds of that House shall agree to pass the Bill, it shall be sent, together with the Objections, to the other House, by which it shall likewise be reconsidered, and if approved by two thirds of that House, it shall become a Law. But in all such Cases the Votes of both Houses shall be determined by Yeas and Nays, and the Names of the Persons voting for and against the Bill shall be entered on the Journal of each House respectively. If any Bill shall not be returned by the President within ten Days (Sundays excepted) after it shall have been presented to him, the Same shall be a Law, in like Manner as if he had signed it, unless the Congress by their Adjournment prevent its Return, in which Case it shall not be a Law.

Every Order, Resolution, or Vote to which the Concurrence of the Senate and House of Representatives may be necessary (except on a question of Adjournment) shall be presented to the President of the United States; and before the Same shall take Effect, shall be approved by him, or being disapproved by him, shall be repassed by two thirds of the Senate and House of Representatives, according to the Rules and Limitations prescribed in the Case of a Bill.

Section 8

The Congress shall have Power To lay and collect Taxes, Duties, Imposts and Excises, to pay the Debts and provide for the common Defence and general Welfare of the United States; but all Duties, Imposts and Excises shall be uniform throughout the United States;

To borrow money on the credit of the United States;

To regulate Commerce with foreign Nations, and among the several States, and with the Indian Tribes;

To establish an uniform Rule of Naturalization, and uniform Laws on the subject of Bankruptcies throughout the United States;

To coin Money, regulate the Value thereof, and of foreign Coin, and fix the Standard of Weights and Measures;

To provide for the Punishment of counterfeiting the Securities and current Coin of the United States;

To establish Post Offices and Post Roads;

To promote the Progress of Science and useful Arts, by securing for limited Times to Authors and Inventors the exclusive Right to their respective Writings and Discoveries;

To constitute Tribunals inferior to the supreme Court;

To define and punish Piracies and Felonies committed on the high Seas, and Offenses against the Law of Nations;

To declare War, grant Letters of Marque and Reprisal, and make Rules concerning Captures on Land and Water;

To raise and support Armies, but no Appropriation of Money to that Use shall be for a longer Term than two Years;

To provide and maintain a Navy;

To make Rules for the Government and Regulation of the land and naval Forces;

To provide for calling forth the Militia to execute the Laws of the Union, suppress Insurrections and repel Invasions;

To provide for organizing, arming, and disciplining, the Militia, and for governing such Part of them as may be employed in the Service of the United States, reserving to the States respectively, the Appointment of the Officers, and the Authority of training the Militia according to the discipline prescribed by Congress;

To exercise exclusive Legislation in all Cases whatsoever, over such District (not exceeding ten Miles square) as may, by Cession of particular States, and the acceptance of Congress, become the Seat of the Government of the United States, and to exercise like Authority over all Places purchased by the Consent of the Legislature of the State in which the Same shall be, for the Erection of Forts, Magazines, Arsenals, dock-Yards, and other needful Buildings; And

To make all Laws which shall be necessary and proper for carrying into Execution the foregoing Powers, and all other Powers vested by this Constitution in the Government of the United States, or in any Department or Officer thereof.

Section 9

The Migration or Importation of such Persons as any of the States now existing shall think proper to admit, shall not be prohibited by the Congress prior to the Year one thousand eight hundred and eight, but a tax or duty may be imposed on such Importation, not exceeding ten dollars for each Person.

The privilege of the Writ of Habeas Corpus shall not be suspended, unless when in Cases of Rebellion or Invasion the public Safety may require it.

No Bill of Attainder or ex post facto Law shall be passed.

No capitation, or other direct, Tax shall be laid, unless in Proportion to the Census or Enumeration herein before directed to be taken.

No Tax or Duty shall be laid on Articles exported from any State.

No Preference shall be given by any Regulation of Commerce or Revenue to the Ports of one State over those of another: nor shall Vessels bound to, or from, one State, be obliged to enter, clear, or pay Duties in another.

No Money shall be drawn from the Treasury, but in Consequence of Appropriations made by Law; and a regular Statement and Account of the Receipts and Expenditures of all public Money shall be published from time to time.

No Title of Nobility shall be granted by the United States: And no Person holding any Office of Profit or Trust under them, shall, without the Consent of the Congress, accept of any present, Emolument, Office, or Title, of any kind whatever, from any King, Prince or foreign State.

Section 10

No State shall enter into any Treaty, Alliance, or Confederation; grant Letters of Marque and Reprisal; coin Money; emit Bills of Credit; make any Thing but gold and silver Coin a Tender in Payment of Debts; pass any Bill of Attainder, ex post facto Law, or Law impairing the Obligation of Contracts, or grant any Title of Nobility.

No State shall, without the Consent of the Congress, lay any Imposts or Duties on Imports or Exports, except what may be absolutely necessary for executing its inspection Laws: and the net Produce of all Duties and Imposts, laid by any State on Imports or Exports, shall be for the Use of the Treasury of the United States; and all such Laws shall be subject to the Revision and Control of the Congress.

No State shall, without the Consent of Congress, lay any duty of Tonnage, keep Troops, or Ships of War in time of Peace, enter into any Agreement or Compact with another State, or with a foreign Power, or engage in War, unless actually invaded, or in such imminent Danger as will not admit of delay.

Article 2.

Section 1

The executive Power shall be vested in a President of the United States of America. He shall hold his Office during the Term of four Years, and, together with the Vice-President chosen for the same Term, be elected, as follows:

Each State shall appoint, in such Manner as the Legislature thereof may direct, a Number of Electors, equal to the whole Number of Senators and Representatives to which the State may be entitled in the Congress: but no Senator or Representative, or Person holding an Office of Trust or Profit under the United States, shall be appointed an Elector.

The Electors shall meet in their respective States, and vote by Ballot for two persons, of whom one at least shall not lie an Inhabitant of the same State with themselves. And they shall make a List of all the Persons voted for, and of the Number of Votes for each; which List they shall sign and certify, and transmit sealed to the Seat of the Government of the United States, directed to the President of the Senate. The President of the Senate shall, in the Presence of the Senate and House of Representatives, open all the Certificates, and the Votes shall then be counted. The Person having the greatest Number of Votes shall be the President, if such Number be a Majority of the whole Number of Electors appointed; and if there be more than one who have such Majority, and have an equal Number of Votes, then the House of Representatives shall immediately choose by Ballot one of them for President; and if no Person have a Majority, then from the five highest on the List the said House shall in like Manner choose the President. But in choosing the President, the Votes shall be taken by States, the Representation from each State having one Vote; a quorum for this Purpose shall consist of a Member or Members from two-thirds of the States, and a Majority of all the States shall be necessary to a Choice. In every Case, after the Choice of the President, the Person having the greatest Number of Votes of the Electors shall be the Vice President. But if there should remain two or more who have equal Votes, the Senate shall choose from them by Ballot the Vice-President.

The Congress may determine the Time of choosing the Electors, and the Day on which they shall give their Votes; which Day shall be the same throughout the United States.

No person except a natural born Citizen, or a Citizen of the United States, at the time of the Adoption of this Constitution, shall be eligible to the Office of President; neither shall any Person be eligible to that Office who shall not have attained to the Age of thirty-five Years, and been fourteen Years a Resident within the United States.

In Case of the Removal of the President from Office, or of his Death, Resignation, or Inability to discharge the Powers and Duties of the said Office, the same shall devolve on the Vice President, and the Congress may by Law provide for the Case of Removal, Death, Resignation or Inability, both of the President and Vice President, declaring what Officer shall then act as President, and such Officer shall act accordingly, until the Disability be removed, or a President shall be elected.

The President shall, at stated Times, receive for his Services, a Compensation, which shall neither be increased nor diminished during the Period for which he shall have been elected, and he shall not receive within that Period any other Emolument from the United States, or any of them.

Before he enter on the Execution of his Office, he shall take the following Oath or Affirmation:

"I do solemnly swear (or affirm) that I will faithfully execute the Office of President of the United States, and will to the best of my Ability, preserve, protect and defend the Constitution of the United States."

Section 2

The President shall be Commander in Chief of the Army and Navy of the United States, and of the Militia of the several States, when called into the actual Service of the United States; he may require the Opinion, in writing, of the principal Officer in each of the executive Departments, upon any subject relating to the Duties of their respective Offices, and he shall have Power to

Grant Reprieves and Pardons for Offenses against the United States, except in Cases of Impeachment.

He shall have Power, by and with the Advice and Consent of the Senate, to make Treaties, provided two thirds of the Senators present concur; and he shall nominate, and by and with the Advice and Consent of the Senate, shall appoint Ambassadors, other public Ministers and Consuls, Judges of the supreme Court, and all other Officers of the United States, whose Appointments are not herein otherwise provided for, and which shall be established by Law: but the Congress may by Law vest the Appointment of such inferior Officers, as they think proper, in the President alone, in the Courts of Law, or in the Heads of Departments.

The President shall have Power to fill up all Vacancies that may happen during the Recess of the Senate, by granting Commissions which shall expire at the End of their next Session.

Section 3

He shall from time to time give to the Congress Information of the State of the Union, and recommend to their Consideration such Measures as he shall judge necessary and expedient; he may, on extraordinary Occasions, convene both Houses, or either of them, and in Case of Disagreement between them, with Respect to the Time of Adjournment, he may adjourn them to such Time as he shall think proper; he shall receive Ambassadors and other public Ministers; he shall take

Care that the Laws be faithfully executed, and shall Commission all the Officers of the United States.

Section 4

The President, Vice President and all civil Officers of the United States, shall be removed from Office on Impeachment for, and Conviction of, Treason, Bribery, or other high Crimes and Misdemeanors.

Article 3.

Section 1

The judicial Power of the United States, shall be vested in one supreme Court, and in such inferior Courts as the Congress may from time to time ordain and establish. The Judges, both of the supreme and inferior Courts, shall hold their Offices during good Behavior, and shall, at stated Times, receive for their Services a Compensation which shall not be diminished during their Continuance in Office.

Section 2

The judicial Power shall extend to all Cases, in Law and Equity, arising under this Constitution, the Laws of the United States, and Treaties made, or which shall be made, under their Authority; to all Cases affecting Ambassadors, other public Ministers and Consuls; to all Cases of admiralty and maritime Jurisdiction; to Controversies to which the United States shall be a

Party; to Controversies between two or more States; between a State and Citizens of another State; between Citizens of different States; between Citizens of the same State claiming Lands under Grants of different States, and between a State, or the Citizens thereof, and foreign States, Citizens or Subjects.

In all Cases affecting Ambassadors, other public Ministers and Consuls, and those in which a State shall be Party, the supreme Court shall have original Jurisdiction. In all the other Cases before mentioned, the supreme Court shall have appellate Jurisdiction, both as to Law and Fact, with such Exceptions, and under such Regulations as the Congress shall make.

The Trial of all Crimes, except in Cases of Impeachment, shall be by Jury; and such Trial shall be held in the State where the said Crimes shall have been committed; but when not committed within any State, the Trial shall be at such Place or Places as the Congress may by Law have directed.

Section 3

Treason against the United States, shall consist only in levying War against them, or in adhering to their Enemies, giving them Aid and Comfort. No Person shall be convicted of Treason unless on the Testimony of two Witnesses to the same overt Act, or on Confession in open Court.

The Congress shall have power to declare the Punishment of Treason, but no Attainder of Treason shall work Corruption of Blood, or Forfeiture except during the Life of the Person attainted.

Article 4.

Section 1

Full Faith and Credit shall be given in each State to the public Acts, Records, and judicial Proceedings of every other State. And the Congress may by general Laws prescribe the Manner in which such Acts, Records and Proceedings shall be proved, and the Effect thereof.

Section 2

The Citizens of each State shall be entitled to all Privileges and Immunities of Citizens in the several States.

A Person charged in any State with Treason, Felony, or other Crime, who shall flee from Justice, and be found in another State, shall on demand of the executive Authority of the State from which he fled, be delivered up, to be removed to the State having Jurisdiction of the Crime.

No Person held to Service or Labour in one State, under the Laws thereof, escaping into another, shall, in Consequence of any Law or Regulation therein, be discharged from such Service or Labour, But shall be delivered up on Claim of the Party to whom such Service or Labour may be due.

Section 3

New States may be admitted by the Congress into this Union; but no new States shall be formed or erected within the Jurisdiction of any other State; nor any State be formed by the Junction of two or more States, or parts of States, without the Consent of the Legislatures of the States concerned as well as of the Congress.

The Congress shall have Power to dispose of and make all needful Rules and Regulations respecting the Territory or other Property belonging to the United States; and nothing in this Constitution shall be so construed as to Prejudice any Claims of the United States, or of any particular State.

Section 4

The United States shall guarantee to every State in this Union a Republican Form of Government, and shall protect each of them against Invasion; and on Application of the Legislature, or of the Executive (when the Legislature cannot be convened) against domestic Violence.

Article 5.

The Congress, whenever two thirds of both Houses shall deem it necessary, shall propose Amendments to this Constitution, or, on the Application of the Legislatures of two thirds of the several States, shall call a Convention for proposing Amendments, which, in either Case, shall be valid to all Intents and Purposes, as part of this Constitution, when ratified by the Legislatures of three fourths the several States, or by Conventions in three fourths thereof, as the one or the other Mode of Ratification may be proposed by the Congress; Provided that no Amendment which may be made prior to the Year One thousand eight hundred and eight shall in any Manner affect the first and fourth Clauses in the Ninth Section of the first Article; and that no State, without its Consent, shall be deprived of its equal Suffrage in the Senate.

Article 6.

All Debts contracted and Engagements entered into, before the Adoption of this Constitution, shall be as valid against the United States under this Constitution, as under the Confederation.

This Constitution, and the Laws of the United States which shall be made in Pursuance thereof; and all Treaties made, or which shall be made, under the Authority of the United States, shall be the supreme Law of the Land; and the Judges in every State shall be bound thereby, any Thing in the Constitution or Laws of any State to the Contrary notwithstanding.

The Senators and Representatives before mentioned, and the Members of the several State Legislatures, and all executive and judicial Officers, both of the United States and of the several States, shall be bound by Oath or Affirmation, to support this Constitution; but no religious Test shall ever be required as a Qualification to any Office or public Trust under the United States.

Article 7.

The Ratification of the Conventions of nine States, shall be sufficient for the Establishment of this Constitution between the States so ratifying the Same.

Done in Convention by the Unanimous Consent of the States present the Seventeenth Day of September in the Year of our Lord one thousand seven hundred and Eighty seven and of the Independence of the United States of America the Twelfth. In Witness whereof We have hereunto subscribed our Names.

George Washington – President and deputy from Virginia

New Hampshire – John Langdon, Nicholas Gilman

Massachusetts – Nathaniel Gorham, Rufus King

Connecticut – William Samuel Johnson, Roger Sherman

New York - Alexander Hamilton

New Jersey – William Livingston, David Brearley, William Paterson, Jonathan Dayton

Pennsylvania – Benjamin Franklin, Thomas Mifflin, Robert Morris, George Clymer, Thomas Fitzsimons, Jared Ingersoll, James Wilson, Gouvernour Morris

Delaware – George Read, Gunning Bedford Jr., John Dickinson, Richard Bassett, Jacob Broom

Maryland – James McHenry, Daniel of St Thomas Jenifer, Daniel Carroll

Virginia – John Blair, James Madison Jr.

North Carolina – William Blount, Richard Dobbs Spaight, Hugh Williamson

South Carolina – John Rutledge, Charles Cotesworth Pinckney, Charles Pinckney, Pierce Butler

Georgia – William Few, Abraham Baldwin

Attest: William Jackson, Secretary

Amendment 1

Congress shall make no law respecting an establishment of religion, or prohibiting the free exercise thereof; or abridging the freedom of speech, or of the press; or the right of the people peaceably to assemble, and to petition the Government for a redress of grievances.

Amendment 2

A well regulated Militia, being necessary to the security of a free State, the right of the people to keep and bear Arms, shall not be infringed.

Amendment 3

No Soldier shall, in time of peace be quartered in any house, without the consent of the Owner, nor in time of war, but in a manner to be prescribed by law.

Amendment 4

The right of the people to be secure in their persons, houses, papers, and effects, against unreasonable searches and seizures, shall not be violated, and no Warrants shall issue, but upon probable cause, supported by Oath or affirmation, and particularly describing the place to be searched, and the persons or things to be seized.

Amendment 5

No person shall be held to answer for a capital, or otherwise infamous crime, unless on a presentment or indictment of a Grand Jury, except in cases arising in the land or naval forces, or in the Militia, when in actual service in time of War or public danger; nor shall any person be subject for the same offense to be twice put in jeopardy of life or limb; nor shall be compelled in any criminal case to be a witness against himself, nor be deprived of life, liberty, or property, without due process of law; nor shall private property be taken for public use, without just compensation.

Amendment 6

In all criminal prosecutions, the accused shall enjoy the right to a speedy and public trial, by an impartial jury of the State and district wherein the crime shall have been committed, which district shall have been previously ascertained by law, and to be informed of the nature and cause of the accusation; to be confronted with the witnesses against him; to have compulsory process for obtaining witnesses in his favor, and to have the Assistance of Counsel for his defence.

Amendment 7

In Suits at common law, where the value in controversy shall exceed twenty dollars, the right of trial by jury shall be preserved, and no fact tried by a jury, shall be otherwise re-examined in any Court of the United States, than according to the rules of the common law.

Amendment 8

Excessive bail shall not be required, nor excessive fines imposed, nor cruel and unusual punishments inflicted.

Amendment 9

The enumeration in the Constitution, of certain rights, shall not be construed to deny or disparage others retained by the people.

Amendment 10

The powers not delegated to the United States by the Constitution, nor prohibited by it to the States, are reserved to the States respectively, or to the people.

Amendment 11

The Judicial power of the United States shall not be construed to extend to any suit in law or equity, commenced or prosecuted against one of the United States by Citizens of another State, or by Citizens or Subjects of any Foreign State.

Amendment 12

The Electors shall meet in their respective states, and vote by ballot for President and Vice-President, one of whom, at least, shall not be an inhabitant of the same state with themselves; they shall name in their ballots the person voted for as President, and in distinct ballots the person voted for as Vice-President, and they shall make distinct lists of all persons voted for as President, and of all persons voted for as Vice-President and of the number of votes for each, which lists they shall sign and certify, and transmit sealed to the seat of the government of the United States, directed to the President of the Senate;

The President of the Senate shall, in the presence of the Senate and House of Representatives, open all the certificates and the votes shall then be counted;

The person having the greatest Number of votes for President, shall be the President, if such number be a majority of the whole number of Electors appointed; and if no person have such majority, then from the persons having the highest numbers not exceeding three on the list of those voted for as President, the House of Representatives shall choose immediately, by ballot, the President. But in choosing the President, the votes shall be taken by states, the representation from each state having one vote; a quorum for this purpose shall consist of a member or members from two-thirds of the states, and a majority of all the states shall be necessary to a choice. And if the House of Representatives shall not choose a President whenever the right of choice shall devolve upon them, before the fourth day of March next following, then the Vice-President shall act as President, as in the case of the death or other constitutional disability of the President.

The person having the greatest number of votes as Vice-President, shall be the Vice-President, if such number be a majority of the whole number of Electors appointed, and if no person have a majority, then from the two highest numbers on the list, the Senate shall choose the

Vice-President; a quorum for the purpose shall consist of two-thirds of the whole number of Senators, and a majority of the whole number shall be necessary to a choice. But no person constitutionally ineligible to the office of President shall be eligible to that of Vice-President of the United States.

Amendment 13

1. Neither slavery nor involuntary servitude, except as a punishment for crime whereof the party shall have been duly convicted, shall exist within the United States, or any place subject to their jurisdiction.

2. Congress shall have power to enforce this article by appropriate legislation.

Amendment 14

1. All persons born or naturalized in the United States, and subject to the jurisdiction thereof, are citizens of the United States and of the State wherein they reside. No State shall make or enforce any law which shall abridge the privileges or immunities of citizens of the United States; nor shall any State deprive any person of life, liberty, or property, without due process of law; nor deny to any person within its jurisdiction the equal protection of the laws.

2. Representatives shall be apportioned among the several States according to their respective numbers, counting the whole number of persons in each State,

excluding Indians not taxed. But when the right to vote at any election for the choice of electors for President and Vice-President of the United States, Representatives in Congress, the Executive and Judicial officers of a State, or the members of the Legislature thereof, is denied to any of the male inhabitants of such State, being twenty-one years of age, and citizens of the United States, or in any way abridged, except for participation in rebellion, or other crime, the basis of representation therein shall be reduced in the proportion which the number of such male citizens shall bear to the whole number of male citizens twenty-one years of age in such State.

3. No person shall be a Senator or Representative in Congress, or elector of President and Vice-President, or hold any office, civil or military, under the United States, or under any State, who, having previously taken an oath, as a member of Congress, or as an officer of the United States, or as a member of any State legislature, or as an executive or judicial officer of any State, to support the Constitution of the United States, shall have engaged in insurrection or rebellion against the same, or given aid or comfort to the enemies thereof. But Congress may by a vote of two-thirds of each House, remove such disability.

4. The validity of the public debt of the United States, authorized by law, including debts incurred for payment of pensions and bounties for services in suppressing insurrection or rebellion, shall not be questioned. But neither the United States nor any State

shall assume or pay any debt or obligation incurred in aid of insurrection or rebellion against the United States, or any claim for the loss or emancipation of any slave; but all such debts, obligations and claims shall be held illegal and void.

5. The Congress shall have power to enforce, by appropriate legislation, the provisions of this article.

Amendment 15

1. The right of citizens of the United States to vote shall not be denied or abridged by the United States or by any State on account of race, color, or previous condition of servitude.

2. The Congress shall have power to enforce this article by appropriate legislation.

Amendment 16

The Congress shall have power to lay and collect taxes on incomes, from whatever source derived, without apportionment among the several States, and without regard to any census or enumeration.

Amendment 17

The Senate of the United States shall be composed of two Senators from each State, elected by the people thereof, for six years; and each Senator shall have one vote.

The electors in each State shall have the qualifications requisite for electors of the most numerous branch of the State legislatures.

When vacancies happen in the representation of any State in the Senate, the executive authority of such State shall issue writs of election to fill such vacancies: Provided, That the legislature of any State may empower the executive thereof to make temporary appointments until the people fill the vacancies by election as the legislature may direct.

This amendment shall not be so construed as to affect the election or term of any Senator chosen before it becomes valid as part of the Constitution.

Amendment 18

1. After one year from the ratification of this article the manufacture, sale, or transportation of intoxicating liquors within, the importation thereof into, or the exportation thereof from the United States and all territory subject to the jurisdiction thereof for beverage purposes is hereby prohibited.

2. The Congress and the several States shall have concurrent power to enforce this article by appropriate legislation.

3. This article shall be inoperative unless it shall have been ratified as an amendment to the Constitution by the legislatures of the several States, as provided in the

Constitution, within seven years from the date of the submission hereof to the States by the Congress.

Amendment 19

The right of citizens of the United States to vote shall not be denied or abridged by the United States or by any State on account of sex.

Congress shall have power to enforce this article by appropriate legislation.

Amendment 20

1. The terms of the President and Vice President shall end at noon on the 20th day of January, and the terms of Senators and Representatives at noon on the 3d day of January, of the years in which such terms would have ended if this article had not been ratified; and the terms of their successors shall then begin.

2. The Congress shall assemble at least once in every year, and such meeting shall begin at noon on the 3d day of January, unless they shall by law appoint a different day.

3. If, at the time fixed for the beginning of the term of the President, the President elect shall have died, the Vice President elect shall become President. If a President shall not have been chosen before the time fixed for the beginning of his term, or if the President elect shall have failed to qualify, then the Vice President elect shall

act as President until a President shall have qualified; and the Congress may by law provide for the case wherein neither a President elect nor a Vice President elect shall have qualified, declaring who shall then act as President, or the manner in which one who is to act shall be selected, and such person shall act accordingly until a President or Vice President shall have qualified.

4. The Congress may by law provide for the case of the death of any of the persons from whom the House of Representatives may choose a President whenever the right of choice shall have devolved upon them, and for the case of the death of any of the persons from whom the Senate may choose a Vice President whenever the right of choice shall have devolved upon them.

5. Sections 1 and 2 shall take effect on the 15th day of October following the ratification of this article.

6. This article shall be inoperative unless it shall have been ratified as an amendment to the Constitution by the legislatures of three-fourths of the several States within seven years from the date of its submission.

Amendment 21

1. The eighteenth article of amendment to the Constitution of the United States is hereby repealed.

2. The transportation or importation into any State, Territory, or possession of the United States for delivery or use therein of intoxicating liquors, in violation of the laws thereof, is hereby prohibited.

3. The article shall be inoperative unless it shall have been ratified as an amendment to the Constitution by conventions in the several States, as provided in the Constitution, within seven years from the date of the submission hereof to the States by the Congress.

Amendment 22

1. No person shall be elected to the office of the President more than twice, and no person who has held the office of President, or acted as President, for more than two years of a term to which some other person was elected President shall be elected to the office of the President more than once. But this Article shall not apply to any person holding the office of President, when this Article was proposed by the Congress, and shall not prevent any person who may be holding the office of President, or acting as President, during the term within which this Article becomes operative from holding the office of President or acting as President during the remainder of such term.

2. This article shall be inoperative unless it shall have been ratified as an amendment to the Constitution by the legislatures of three-fourths of the several States within seven years from the date of its submission to the States by the Congress.

Amendment 23

1. The District constituting the seat of Government of the United States shall appoint in such manner as the

Congress may direct: A number of electors of President and Vice President equal to the whole number of Senators and Representatives in Congress to which the District would be entitled if it were a State, but in no event more than the least populous State; they shall be in addition to those appointed by the States, but they shall be considered, for the purposes of the election of President and Vice President, to be electors appointed by a State; and they shall meet in the District and perform such duties as provided by the twelfth article of amendment.

2. The Congress shall have power to enforce this article by appropriate legislation.

Amendment 24

1. The right of citizens of the United States to vote in any primary or other election for President or Vice President, for electors for President or Vice President, or for Senator or Representative in Congress, shall not be denied or abridged by the United States or any State by reason of failure to pay any poll tax or other tax.

2. The Congress shall have power to enforce this article by appropriate legislation.

Amendment 25

1. In case of the removal of the President from office or of his death or resignation, the Vice President shall become President.

2. Whenever there is a vacancy in the office of the Vice President, the President shall nominate a Vice President who shall take office upon confirmation by a majority vote of both Houses of Congress.

3. Whenever the President transmits to the President pro tempore of the Senate and the Speaker of the House of Representatives his written declaration that he is unable to discharge the powers and duties of his office, and until he transmits to them a written declaration to the contrary, such powers and duties shall be discharged by the Vice President as Acting President.

4. Whenever the Vice President and a majority of either the principal officers of the executive departments or of such other body as Congress may by law provide, transmit to the President pro tempore of the Senate and the Speaker of the House of Representatives their written declaration that the President is unable to discharge the powers and duties of his office, the Vice President shall immediately assume the powers and duties of the office as Acting President.

Thereafter, when the President transmits to the President pro tempore of the Senate and the Speaker of the House of Representatives his written declaration that no inability exists, he shall resume the powers and duties of his office unless the Vice President and a majority of either the principal officers of the executive department or of such other body as Congress may by law provide, transmit within four days to the President pro tempore of the Senate and the Speaker of the House of Representatives their written declaration that the President is unable to discharge the powers and duties of his office. Thereupon Congress shall decide the issue, assembling within forty-eight hours for that purpose if not in session. If the Congress, within twenty-one days after receipt of the latter written declaration, or, if Congress is not in session, within twenty-one days after Congress is required to assemble, determines by two thirds vote of both Houses that the President is unable to discharge the powers and duties of his office, the Vice President shall continue to discharge the same as Acting President; otherwise, the President shall resume the powers and duties of his office.

Amendment 26

1. The right of citizens of the United States, who are eighteen years of age or older, to vote shall not be denied or abridged by the United States or by any State on account of age.

2. The Congress shall have power to enforce this article by appropriate legislation.

Amendment 27

No law, varying the compensation for the services of the Senators and Representatives, shall take effect, until an election of Representatives shall have intervened.

O'Leary Publishing provides concierge book publishing services for brands, professionals, and entrepreneurs. We bring you from idea to print effortlessly through a proven system that is especially effective for non-writers and those who would prefer to leave the writing to an expert. For more about our services visit www.olearypublishing.com.

The O'Leary Publishing Team

CPSIA information can be obtained
at www.ICGtesting.com
Printed in the USA
JSHW011112200220
4311JS00001B/5